Him, Her & Me

Mary Hayley Bell

Him, Her & Me

The Autobiography of Mr Chips, A Yorkshire Terrier

with drawings by Molly Blake

Weidenfeld and Nicolson · London

First published in Great Britain by
George Weidenfeld & Nicolson Ltd,
91 Clapham High Street, London sw4 7TA
1981

Book design by Joyce Chester

ISBN 0 297 77956 7

Set, printed and bound in Great Britain by
Fakenham Press Limited,
Fakenham, Norfolk

Contents

The little dog laughed
To see such craft,
While the dish ran after the spoon.

1 Early Escapades

My name is Mr Chips. I'm a Yorkshire Terrier. Not a Toy, mind you. I weigh seven pounds and I'm twenty-one inches long. I'm lively, alert, on my toes, with a keen outlook on life – which doesn't mean soft and sweet like a Toy with its hair done up in a ribbon. They tried a rubber-band on my hair once, but I soon got rid of that.

As for my general appearance ... my coat hangs straight and evenly from a centre parting down my back, glossy like silk; mind you, it's a bit wonky at the moment as They will insist on giving me a poodle-cut in the summer and every intelligent person knows that if you keep cutting hair it's apt to become curly, which I hate. My eyes are medium dark and sparkling, with a very intelligent expression, though I say it myself. I'm dark steel-blue from back of skull to root of tail, and the hair on my chest is a rich, bright tan, like the hair on my legs. You could call me cute. I don't mean 'cute cute' as the Americans term it – I mean dead on the ball.

I'm very proud of my family. My great-grandfather was a champion. He was called Beechrise Superb. I never knew what his pet name was because my mother never told me and I never saw him, of course. My father, whom my mother told me I resembled, was called Aimhigh Pearly Chip. She was registered as Inskool – Jamboree Home Inskool. What a name! She was usually referred to as 'You', which I think fairly derogatory.

I'm telling you all this for starters. Everyone in this house

where I live is at it: I mean painting or cooking, just plain
reading or writing their autobiographies, so I thought, why
shouldn't I write mine? Mean to say, there's not much else to
do. She washes up, cooks, waters the flowers She grows in the
greenhouse and feeds all those idiotic birds and squirrels. He
is always stuck up in His room writing His memoirs. My walks
have become more feeble every day; I'm lucky to get nine holes
on the golf course, where She sends Him out for air. I'm pretty
good at my kind of golf. I mean to say, I don't chew up the balls
like I used to when I first came here. Once I chewed twenty-five
balls in one day, but He put a stop to that. Now I just sit down
and let Him find His own balls, burrowing about in the undergrowth, while I wait by His trolley. I had to pay Him back
somehow. At least I'm the only dog allowed in the club-house,
though I wish I could reach the fruit-machine – they all seem to
have such fun on that thing.

I'd better get on with my story before I go off the whole idea. I
was born in this home called Jamboree. It was a pretty good
place. There was every imaginable kind of dog there – fifteen
different breeds, I was told by my mother. The lady who ran it
was great, really great; she cared for you, however small you
were, and I'm small. Have to admit it.

Then one day these two arrived. They were searching for an
Alsatian. Well, I was in a tub at the time with several others of
my own breed. We were parked in a doorway. It was freezing. I
was four months old. I liked the look of Them. They had a nice
car for a start and I particularly liked Him. I sort of knew Him.
Maybe I'd seen Him on some film or other in the house. He
didn't say much, but kept looking around, quietly.

She went through the lot. She was after a Cocker Spaniel, she
said, changing her mind, as They'd always had them; but none
of the Cockers seemed to appeal – they just stared at Her, put
Her off. Then She was on about this English Setter, then this
Scottish Setter; then She thought they'd eat too much. Really!
Talking of food . . . well, I'll go on to that later. Mean to say I *am*
a Yorkshire Terrier, and we get through a lot of energy. No one
knows where we originated from as a race, but my mother told

me we drifted from Scotland to Yorkshire. Our ancestors were sporting people and were put to fight monkeys and rats in the 1800s, and Huddersfield Ben, one of the first of our breed born in 1865, was a great expert at bull-baiting.

So, She went through all fifteen breeds again and there wasn't an Alsatian there anyway. She kept on about a guard dog. Then She said She was dead keen on the Scottish Setter. I have to admit he was pretty gorgeous to look at. I kept grinning and carrying on alarmingly.

Then They went away! I collapsed into the tub.

'They always come back,' someone said to me. 'Always.'

'But She wants this Setter!'

'It's sold, stupid!'

'Oh.'

I liked the look of Them, I did really, and the car. I thought They might have a pretty nice little house somewhere, maybe with a bit of a garden.

'It'll be a patio in London if you're lucky,' one of the others said.

I kept an eye out for them for a couple of days, though it seemed like weeks. I've never had any idea of time.

They came back. I was still in this wretched tub with about four others. I saw to it I was in a good position. Standing on someone's head I had a good view. To my horror I saw that it was another couple who definitely were after one of us. I crouched in the bottom of the tub and tried to look really *sick*. Closed my eyes and fell asleep. These people picked up all the others, like slaves really, but I was definitely a write-off. Saved! They went off with one of the others. I often wonder if she went to a patio in London, wherever that is.

When He and She finally did come back, She was still going on about this Setter, wanting to be told when another arrived. I saw Him coming towards me. I stood on this chap's head and did everything in the book to catch His attention. He stopped and looked at me. I looked at Him and wagged my tail furiously. He picked me out of the tub. I licked him like hell all over.

The Jamboree lady smiled: 'Once anyone has a Yorkie', she said, 'they never want anything else. They're great companions, they never moult, they don't eat too much, very affectionate, and as good a house dog as an Alsatian for warning you; also, if they get hold of an intruder, they bite his ankles.' (Remember that, I thought, wherever his ankles are.)

'Darling,' He said, 'I really love this little character.'

'Really?' She said and looked away. I could have killed Her.

'Don't forget how often we have to go away; he'd be so easy to park with someone.'

Park, I wondered. What's their game?

'He *is* rather sweet, but I wanted a real dog,' She said. Real dog? She had to be mad.

'You won't regret him,' the Jamboree lady said.

'I really love him,' He said, and I believed Him, and I always have, even when He called me a caterpillar.

'Then, let's have him darling.' *Saved!*

'What shall we call him?' He asked.

'Well, his father was called Aimhigh Pearly Chip,' said the dear Jamboree lady.

'Chips,' He said, 'after a film I was in called *Goodbye Mr Chips*.'

'Chips,' She said. 'I like that.'

They bundled me into this car and, though I felt exceedingly sick, I never showed it.

Well, we arrived at this house. *House!* It was the biggest place I'd ever seen – naturally, as I came out of this tub crammed with at least six bodies. It seemed *enormous*. I really lost myself in all those rooms. Of course now I know them all and wander around where I please. Beds I like, especially the bed in the spare room, as They call it. It's huge, and one can roll around on the eiderdown. I get ticked off by Her, and put in what She calls 'Disgrace Corner', which is behind the sofa in the library. Actually, I like it: you can lie on your back and stick your legs up on the wall.

But, to continue. Apart from the size of the house, there is what They call the garden, which literally goes on forever in all directions. Mean to say, there is the 'Garden with the Golden Caterpillar Tree', where they lie around in the hot months, the 'Azalea Garden', the 'Vegetable Garden' with Sweet Peas in it, and the 'Orchard', which I must admit is really *something* when all the fruit blossom is out, though I don't personally go for fruit. He does, though; He just crams in apples by the dozen.

Well, I was taken into this immense piece of land and shown to this man called Harold. He's a tame gardener. Well, you see, he did quite the wrong thing as far as I was concerned. Mean to say, the garden was frightening enough, but this weirdo made ludicrous advances towards me, pointing his fingers and making noises – trying to be funny, of course – but in my view talking down to me, if you get my meaning. I barked like crazy, and they all laughed. Actually, I've really grown to like Harold, though I never lose the opportunity of barking at him, even if he's only minding his own business. He doesn't speak Dog, so I can say what I like to him, and I do.

He's always telling Them that he can't understand me, because when he takes me out for a walk when They're not around, I'm 'as good as gold', he says. If, or should I say when, he takes me to The Swan, I get up on his lap and am 'good as gold'. Of course I am, because there's a purpose in all that from my point of view – we get to go into this graveyard, which is really nice, with all those stones to leak on ... then on to The Swan, where they're always munching some kind of sandwich.

I definitely like Harold; *he*'s 'good as gold'. I like watching him. He's always busy, digging things in and then digging them up, putting sticks in, then cutting them down. It astonishes me. He puts something in the ground and, a few weeks later, whatever they are, they all shoot up. Mean to say, I have to admire these things they all call Sweet Peas; how he gets all those things to smell I'll never know, and the colours! I often just sit in the middle of them to enjoy the smell; but he doesn't go for that and waves a great broom at me to move off. Don't ask me why. Then he collects mountains of leaves for no good reason and, believe it or believe it not, he carts the whole lot off on this tractor thing called a Wheel Horse – well, it's got wheels but, if it's a horse, it's a horse with no head – then he takes the leaves to the end of the orchard, and sets them all on fire. It amazes me the things these Humans get up to.

That reminds me. I've learned that it's all divided into three ways of life. There are Animals, Birds and Humans, in that order, and they're all themselves. Take this squirrel: he's called Fred, apparently. They found him when he was very small. He'd fallen out of his nest as a baby, so They put him in prison and fed him. Personally I thought he was a rat, an under-privileged rat whom I couldn't wait to get hold of, but She said I couldn't. They fed him on nuts and one day Crispian, who is what They call a Grand Son, let him out. Well, I would have thought he'd have scuttled off. I tried to catch him, but he can climb a tree, and he does, and it's one of the things I can't do.

Harold was pretty sad about the whole episode; though no one admitted to letting Fred out.

'Don't worry, Harold,' She said. 'He'll be back.'

Harold shook his head mournfully. He has a funny habit of snatching his woolly cap off his head every time he sees Her.

Well, will you believe it, this deprived rat did come back, every day. And Harold fed him, and so did She, with these nuts he likes. They used to give them to him with Their fingers until, one day, he bit through Her thumb-nail. Now They just throw these things on the floor. At first he used to scurry off and bury them all over the garden – how he knew where to find them again I'll never know – but now it's winter, and though She told me he should have hibernated, whatever that is, he didn't. Every day he's around, waiting for these nuts. I tried one or two while he was off hiding another lot, and as far as I'm concerned he can keep them all.

That brings me back to the three ways of life. She has this bird table, you see. Several times each day she puts toast and bread and nuts, even meat sometimes, on it. I have to admit that I do get up on it when there's meat. All these birds swarm in and get at it. There are these doves called Koo Koo for no reason, tits, endless sparrows, and the ones She calls Bovver Boys who are really starlings, and some quite beautifully coloured ones, bullfinches, greater spotted nuthatches, and a woodpecker – chaps who are pretty elusive. Magpies, jays, fly-catchers – you name them, they're all here. I watch them discreetly through the window from the back of the sofa. They gobble everything up like there is no tomorrow. But when Fred appears with his two friends, Georgie and the Marauder, who really *is* a rat with a rotten tail, they all sit around like idiots and let these characters eat up everything! Which goes to show that Animals are above Birds. I have to say that Birds are sycophants, especially this Robin, who is beautiful but stupid most of the time.

Sometimes I'm told to see this Marauder off, but so far I've missed him because my wretched hair gets in my eyes and I lose his scent. This bird called Robin, who sits on the rose tree, is the only one who is allowed to share the bird table with Fred. They must have something in common I don't know about. Mean to say, Fred actually sits on the doorstep waiting to be fed, and personally I think She and Harold are a bit intimidated by him, because they always search their pockets wildly and fling out these nuts. He's compelling, that's what he is. Why, even today, he walked into the drawing-room bold as brass and helped himself to the nuts on the table kept for the Humans – they eat them too when they drink this stuff out of bottles and laugh a lot. As far as I'm concerned, he knows I'm a bigger Animal than he is and that I should be avoided. He never speaks to me, so I can't get his angle on life. He just glares at me with his beady eyes. One day I *will* get him, but then there will be murder from Him and Her, so I'm waiting until he gets into the orchard.

A great many people come to this house, mostly they go when they've finished their coffee in the kitchen, that's when I hear them talking about the others – they're called famous, or 'very important people' – but I don't know who they are. Some come often, so I know them well. There are two Dickies, one has a wife called Ha Ha, and the other has a wife called Scrubber. I like them. Then there's another man who tells funny stories and makes them all laugh a lot, he's just called Larry; he has a wife, too, called Plugright. A fat man I wasn't too keen on, was so enormous that when he sat on this chair it broke. I went for him in the dining-room, and there was a bit of a scene as a few things fell off the table.

Harold is the one in the kitchen. I like him, as I said. He's been here all my life. He's called the 'salt of the earth', whatever that means. Perhaps it's because he can do practically everything like cutting wood, mending things and lighting fires, not only in the house, but at the bonfire. The fire he lights in the study, near Disgrace Corner, is so huge and hot that sometimes I wonder if he's trying to burn Them to death.

Then there are also these Humans that they call the 'Royals': Elizabeth and Margaret, who come and shove this hoover thing about. I love Margaret; I really love them both. Margaret is mostly in the laundry room and the kitchen. She put this endless amount of washing in a rather fearsome box which roars away. Next, she tells me, the washing goes to a thing called a spin-drier, and then a tumble-drier if it's not hot and sunny. But, if it's hot and sunny, it all hangs on a rope between two cherry trees to get the air, but He doesn't like the look of it because it reminds Him of years ago when He said you had to fight your way through them to get anywhere, like when They were all Children and the napkins froze in the frost and were like hard boards. Sometimes I sit on Margaret's foot when she's ironing so as to stop her. I like her hair, it's all bunched up on the top of her head, like a huge special nest. I'm always expecting birds to peer out, but so far I haven't seen any.

Elizabeth is really lovely. She's Russian, whatever that is; she has long black hair and strange eyes, and it is through her that I met Tina. Tina is a Yorkshire Terrier too, and simply gorgeous. She's my wife now and we have five children. I'll get on to that later, but I may as well tell you that when I first saw those five squirming things I felt quite nauseated. They were brought over in a basket. Tina edged up to me.

'Keep right away from them,' she said. 'Right away.' So I went into Disgrace Corner, and everyone laughed.

'Come on, Chips,' He said. 'They're your children.' He dragged me out.

'Keep well away,' said Tina. 'Turn your back on them. I don't want you biting my babies.'

I turned my back. They all laughed again. Actually, when I spent the weekend with Elizabeth and they crawled all over me, I *did* bite them. Extraordinary really. I remembered the tub and how I must have been like that myself once. I just hope none of them comes here to stay, but I've got a nasty feeling one of them one day just *may* land up here. I found them pretty pushy and I could see all my favourite places being taken – oh, well!

Where was I? Ah yes, my beginnings. I thoroughly enjoyed my early days. They made a great fuss of me. I had a huge basket, which had belonged once to someone called Hamlet. He was a Cocker Spaniel, so you can imagine how big it was. Also, They had a white sheepskin rug, which moulted all over Their brown carpet, so They put it in my basket! I luxuriated in it and told myself to forget the former inhabitant, who was dead. He was run over and She had been mad about him. They surrounded this basket with newspaper upon which I was supposed to leak – something I did occasionally, when not reading the large print.

She goes shopping quite often, and some lugubrious twerp told Her to carry me in Her shopping basket. I decided from the start that this was not on. I am not going to be carted about in a shopping basket like the Toys, who have their hair done up in a ribbon on the top of their heads. In a curious way I decided to emulate Hamlet and be a Big Dog, which in point of fact I've proved I am, because I can do eighteen holes of golf. She pretty soon learned that I was not for shopping. Gerrards Cross to me is unutterable hell . . . all those huge feet coming at me, and the wheels of cars, and the *noise* in the shops! Wow!

Because He liked to take me with Him, I allowed myself to go on this lead, which, on several occasions, nearly hanged me. A couple of times I saw really big dogs tied to a lamp-post while the boss went shopping, sitting there like idiotic fools, no dignity, waiting endlessly. I just pulled Him along at a great pace, tearing through these legs. Once I collided with an Old Human, who got the lead caught in his trousers and he collapsed. Another time I bellowed into a Labrador's ear, 'You must be unhinged to sit tied to a lamp-post like that. Are you for sale or something?' He kicked me. The Humans all smiled at each other and thought we were getting on fine. Actually, what he said was, 'You miserable little runt.'

Now I positively refuse to go to Gerrards Cross. I hate it. It's either full of these car wheels or huge legs or these tomfool dogs tied to lamp-posts. Now and again you even see these strutting ladies hauled along by a huge dog *carrying* the basket or a newspaper. Not me! I just sit in the car, behind the wheel, like I'm driving – like someone in possession of their faculties.

Pubs I like. I'm off the hook there. The legs are mostly hanging from these stools and don't get in my way if I'm sniffing out another dog to say something rude to; or the occasional cat, who is either completely unimpressed or a spitfire with a nasty pair of claws and to be avoided unless I want to lose an eye, which I don't.

My idea of complete heaven is the golf course. There, there is only Him and me, and whoever He's playing a game with. It's a whole world up there. The sky comes right down to it, and I'm as free as the only people I envy – the Birds. She doesn't come up there to play golf. She goes up for Sunday lunch sometimes, and they all whack into this beef. On these occasions I'm not allowed in the club-house. They used to tie me to an old umbrella stand or foot cleaner, but I got wise to that, remembering those undignified dogs in Gerrards Cross, so now I stay in the car and watch them muffing their shots on the first tee. Golly, if I could get a small enough club in my paws I'd show them, I really would. Anyone can do it – *anyone*.

Sunday lunch is quite fun and very efficacious for me because She always brings out a Doggy Bag, which means She took too much food and couldn't eat it, so I get it. Can't grumble about that.

They both have letters after their name: She has JP and He has CBE. Imagine my delight when, one day, she put a tag round my neck and on it was MCP. I was really chuffed, particularly as I thought I'd got away with attacking Mr Nagel, the grocer. I lunged at him from a sitting position, so I just about got him in the hip before he escaped.

I don't know what it is about Mr Nagel. No one could be more 'obliging', She says; but, when I see him, I lose control. It's the same with the milkman or the chap from Fortnum & Mason, or the laundry. As for the burglar-alarm man, I really got him: he had to be dealt with – sticking plaster and Dettol. I dunno, it's something in my subconscious that I can't quite remember.

I think I'll talk to Mimi about it. She's staying with us now, with this girl called Melodie. She – I mean Mimi – is a hundred years old, but *really* all there. I admire her. I have to. I went to her room and pinched a bone out of her basket. I'm not allowed bones on account of the fact that I'm inclined to bury them under bulbs, particularly one called Alstromeria. Anyway, I was caught dodging between Her legs and Harold's, who of course pointed out the fact that I was carrying it to a private place. It was removed from my mouth and I was ticked off. Livid, I went back to Mimi's basket while she was taking a walk on the lawn, and I'm ashamed to say I was tempted into eating up her fish whiskers, which I really enjoyed. Melodie found out and told. Well! That's when I was given this tag round my neck with these letters, MCP. I thought it was just one of those dates when you get to have a ribbon stuck on you for bravery, birthdays and Christmas. I showed it to Mimi.

'I've been decorated,' I said. 'I'm on the Honours List.' And I showed her this medal thing. She regarded it with a sniff. She sniffs a lot. All Pekinese dogs do; don't ask me why.

'MCP,' she said.

'I know. I can read!' I replied.

'What does it mean?' she asked.

'Not sure,' I answered, 'but it has to be something important. Mean to say, they've both got tags like this, even if you don't see them actually wearing them, like I do. Mine has just been donated.'

'Ah,' she said.

'What does that mean?'

'What does what mean?'

'What does that mean – Ah?'

'You'd better sit down,' she said.

I did so. We were alone in the garage. She gazed at me with her large brown eyes for a moment or two.

'Now, look here,' she said slowly, 'I'm nearly a hundred years old and I've been through a lot, seen a lot and heard a lot. You may think I'm a boring old Peke...'

'I never said that...'

'But it so happens that I'm very wise.'

'I know you are.'

'I come from China, which is older than Yorkshire by a very long chalk.'

'So?'

'And I know what MCP means.'

'You do?' I asked eagerly.

'I do.'

'Well?'

'I don't think you're going to like your Medal.'

'Why not? Why *not*?'

'Because it's something given to animals that have not been very nice about something.' She scratched her long ears.

'What do you mean?' I queried.

'Well, eating my fish whiskers...'

'Oh, that...'

'Worse, trying to bite poor Mr Nagel, who's lame!'

'I'm lame too. If you want to know, I'll tell you my experiences about being lame.'

'No excuse. What about F and M, the laundry man, the milkman, Harold! And anyway you're not as lame as you make out. I know, I've watched you – from the window.'

'Oh... that's just a bit of fun. Never mind that now. I want to know about my medal which She stuck on me. Go on, tell me.'

She regarded me quite sternly for a second or two. She has these long nails covered in long soft hairs, and she picked at them.

'Mimi!' I shouted. 'What does MCP *mean*?'

'It means,' she said deliberately, 'Male Chauvinist Pig.'

I stared at her. She went on.

'It's about the nastiest thing you can say about a human, let alone an animal!'

My lower jaw dropped. She nodded knowingly.

'Get it off then, get it *off* me!' I shouted.

'I haven't got enough teeth,' she said, and swept into the kitchen.

I fought to get this tag off; I crashed against the wall of the garage. Mean to say, I really *injured* myself, but I couldn't reach it. I sat down in a sweat. They came out. He was going to golf, and She was seeing him off.

'Golf, Chips?' She said.

I closed my eyes. With this tag on me? No thanks. I lay on my back hopelessly, helplessly.

'He doesn't want that luggage label on him now,' He said, and took it off. Then He read it aloud: 'MCP. First Class.'

I crawled into the back of his car and sat there with my eyes closed. They laughed. I could have killed Them both.

2 A Brave Yorkshireman

I DIDN'T FEEL very well that night. I spent most of the time in Disgrace Corner. As a breed we're easily hurt, and I was. They kept feeling my nose and cuddling me. It wasn't any good. I didn't even go up to bed with Them. Upstairs, I have the choice of two places, either a smallish basket or this blanket under His bedside table, where you have to sleep on about a hundred different wires – the Teasmade wire, the electric clock wire, the toaster, the kettle and the phone wire. One day, She says, I'll be electrocuted, whatever that is; but usually I sleep pretty well there, until about 7 a.m. when this Teasmaking thing begins to hiss; then I get up on the bed – His side, not Hers because she kicks me off.

Anyway, I did not go upstairs that night. Mimi's words had sunk in deep. Male Chauvinist Pig. What the heck Chauvinist means I'll never know, but *Pig*! That slew me, particularly as she was up in her room and I couldn't get her to explain. I thought They liked me. I certainly showed I *loved* them. How could They go and pin that tag on me?

I slept in the kitchen. I clambered into my big basket with the white sheepskin rug. It comforted me. He put the burglar alarm on and I was shut in the kitchen. (I've never understood this burglar alarm. I imagine it's a huge creature who sits in the broom cupboard, and if anyone walks about after the trolley is put in front of the hall step, he lets out a piercing scream. One day They'll let him out and he'll get me. I know that. So I stay put.)

I drank some water; it hadn't been changed and tasted stale. Then I munched a bit of this awful tinned stuff they give me. I used to tolerate it until I stayed with Elizabeth and she introduced me to a delicious stuff called ox heart. Now They're forced to give me ox heart, though She still mixes in some of this tinned stuff as well. A friend of mine in the poodle parlour where we get our hair cut in the summer told me not to believe what I see on television about animal food. 'I can't look at the telly anyway,' I said. 'It makes me nervous.'

'Well,' my friend said, 'you'll see all sizes and shapes of dogs devouring this tinned stuff as though there were no tomorrow, but I've heard that these wretches are starved for forty-eight hours beforehand, and the truth is that they'd even eat a rubber glove by then.'

One thing I do not like is other dogs in my house. I hear people say what good manners they have, but actually they don't: the first thing they do is rush to the kitchen and eat up my food.

I got back into bed. Then I remembered I hadn't had my last leak. I did it under the kitchen table, so that it looked as if it had come from the washing machine. Male Chauvinist Pig First Class ... I couldn't forget it. 'They're very sensitive dogs, Yorkies,' He said once. We most certainly are, even though we don't come from China.

I couldn't sleep. I wished I had a Mogadon. He has it sometimes when He can't sleep. 'Can I have a Mogadon please, darling?' He'll say. Then He gollops it down with some water in a glass. I looked round the kitchen but, as I don't know what Mogadon looks like, I never found it. A mouse came up and looked at me. I couldn't be bothered. I closed my eyes. I was pretty certain he wouldn't come any nearer...

After a while I fell asleep. It was the oddest thing. I went right back to my beginnings in that tub. Back to this big old place as I first saw it. Heard these crashing church bells, saw this giant garden and all this velvet grass, the blossom on the trees, the endless daffodils standing to attention, trees that touched the sky, flowers everywhere, listening to Her talking to them, these two ghouls in the tree, the Koo Koos. Harold in his brown cap and overgrown boots and Himself on this terrifying thing called a Wheel Horse, which had no head and never did any droppings.

I smiled in my sleep. Then, all of a sudden, things changed and my dream turned into a nightmare. I was edging down these wide stairs. There was a Human putting a lock on a door. I went up to him, friendly like, and he stood on my right arm. I screamed and screamed. She came rushing from the kitchen and scooped me up in her arms.

'What happened?' she asked.

This Human turned his head and said straight out: 'Well, he was coming down the stairs carrying a bone, he must have tripped on it and hurt hisself.'

'Liar!' I shrieked. 'I never had a bone, and if I had I would have been more than capable of carrying it down these wide stairs!'

'There, there, poor baby,' She said.

But I went on yelling. The pain was beyond description. She wrapped me up in some old blanket, but I never stopped screaming. Must have been hours. Till He came home.

'We must take him to a vet,' He said.

'Vet? What's a vet?' I bellowed.

We all got into this car and went for miles! I screamed all the way until I couldn't any more.

'He's feeling better,' She said.

'You idiot,' I shouted, 'I've just lost my voice, that's what I've done, lost my voice!'

This vet was a Human in a long white coat. We sat in a room. There were other dogs there.

'Shut up!' This German sausage dog said.

I was too exhausted to listen and started crying, really crying.

'Don't be such a baby,' an Alsatian said. He had a boil on his nose. I knew all these characters, because I'd seen them all in

Jamboree. There was another thing in a basket with a lid on that I didn't want to know about, and something else with a bandaged head that might have been *anything* . . .

This Human in the long white coat called us in. He stuck me on this table and started fumbling with my leg. I started screaming again.

'I think he's just ricked it,' he said. 'I'll give him something to make him sleep.'

Something! He stuck a great needle into my behind and I passed out, but not before I saw all these grinning dogs as I was carried out . . .

I stirred in my sleep and half woke up in the old basket. My leg was killing me all over again. The memory, I suppose. I looked round. The kitchen was still there. I fell asleep again. D'you think this nightmare went away? Not on your nelly. I was back in it . . .

Now we were in some place called Billingshurst – don't ask me where it is. I do know They were very worried; irritated too, I think. They kept giving me pills. I suppose they were Mogadon. I was half asleep most of the time and couldn't walk, even when a nice human in some uniform carried me out and stuck me on the grass. I just about managed that . . . Then we went to this big old barn called a theatre. He was doing the acting. She was dressing him as if He was a ruddy baby.

Then this really kind human came in, called Duncan. I'll always remember him. He had hair all over his face, and looked rather like a St Bernard. He was very concerned, I could see that. He had a friend called Les. Between them they took me in an excruciatingly uncomfy vehicle to another vet.

I was nearly bananas by this time. The vet had a good look at my arm. 'It's broken,' he said. Just that: 'It's broken.' Then he stuck two bits of wood on either side so that the leg stuck out in front of me. It hurt like hell and I screamed some more. Out came this great needle and was stuck into my behind again. I collapsed. My last thought was that I wished I was back in the tub and had never seen any of them.

I must have slept for days. When my senses returned, I found myself in this bedroom. They were both in bed asleep. I had a good look at myself. I really looked a proper Charlie. My front right leg stuck straight out in front of me. To walk I had to hop on three legs. I was in a permanent Heil Hitler position, and I can tell you I didn't go for it. However, being a Yorkshireman, I wasn't going to be beaten. I just hopped around everywhere; even went sideways down these wide stairs. I remember a lot of people about, carrying on about 'the poor little thing' and that sort of stuff. I got a lot of nice pieces of meat given to me in the room, and I just sat down and read His golf magazine.

He's pretty keen on golf, and quite good, I suppose. But golf seems to mean you just stare down at this little white ball and then take a great hack at it and it goes for miles and then you have to chase it. Idiotic really. 'A good walk spoiled,' She says, and I agree. Though I really enjoy it – the walk, I mean.

Well, He took me with Him to this new golf course. I will never forget the horror of it. He was very kind lifting me over ditches and that, but I felt I had to put a good face on it all and I followed Him *everywhere* – up hills, down hills, on to these things called 'greens', where this flag shows you where the hole is that this wretched ball has to go into. You can sit down there because it seems to take forever to get this silly ball into this small hole.

It was raining on top of everything else. I was soaked. I looked like a rat, I really did! And this stupid splint stuck out in front of me was covered with mud and stuff. But I wasn't going to be beaten, so I kept going on my three pins with this arm stuck out in front of me. Sometimes I tripped over it, but I managed *eighteen* of these holes! He was pretty chuffed. He really was. He told Her I was a terrific sport. A great character, that's what He called me.

Don't think this was the end of my nightmare, because it wasn't. We came home at last. They weren't happy about this splint so, believe it or believe it not, I went to another vet!

I didn't like his approach to the whole situation.

'I'll have to put a steel pin in his arm,' that's what he said.
I screamed the house down. He was a very gentle man. I
liked him. He talked to me all the time. Then he stuck a huge
great needle into me again and I passed out.

When I woke up I was in prison. Yes, Prison. I was in a sort of
rabbit hutch full of straw, there was some kind of yard in front of
me and wire all round it. It was dark. There wasn't a sign of
anyone. I had to keep telling myself that They wouldn't have
deserted me in prison. Mean to say, what crime had I
committed? It was that character at the bottom of the stairs. He
should have been stuck in this rabbit hutch. I was the victim!

I managed to struggle out into the yard and take a leak and
then I hopped round to scrutinize this wire. There was no way
out. I went back to this rabbit hutch and I have to confess that I
just sat down and cried myself to sleep. I don't know how long I
was there. It seemed forever, but there was nothing I could do
but wait.

I waited. I was fed by a nice lady. But where were *They*? I
never saw another dog, nor a cat even. I was glad about that, for
any cat would have got the better of me in my condition. I must
have lost pounds in my anxiety.

At last They came! I was hysterical. I was almost delirious. I
was at my lowest ebb. I was almost prepared to kill myself, but
couldn't figure out how to do it. They took me back to this
lovely old velvety garden, and my Special Place, and kept
telling everyone how brave I was, on account of now I had a
steel pin in my elbow. Can you imagine? I just hoped it wasn't
going to go bad inside me or mess up my physical life.

Well, I don't think it did, though you can now call me lame –
like Mr Nagel – which makes me wonder why I want to go for
him, because we're both in the same boat, but I don't quite
understand it all. I do know for certain that at last I understand
about vets, and about ankles. Every Human man I see is to me a
potential vet, nice or nasty. I just *have* to go for their ankles,
which of course means their trousers.

I'm warned off every time these bells go, you know, front or
back door. Occasionally I let them pass me by, but when this

chap with the drink comes I let him have it. Wouldn't you, if someone referred to you as an 'oral obstacle'? Really!

The nightmare passed. I was in my Special Place. The splint had long since gone. The nasty tag had gone, too. I just hoped no one would refer to it again. Even Mimi, that old Chinese Empress. Mind you, I admire her: her age, and the way she sits up in Melodie's room on this throne-like chair all muffled in cushions for hours. She does walk about a bit, but too slowly for any fun.

Know something? I'd call this a nervous house. I know *I* get very nervous with this thing called television. Mean to say, if I could look at it I might understand, but I can't. The noise is terrible: everyone seems to be shooting guns at everyone else, or someone is screaming what she likes to call music. I get into a panic and keep asking to leave the room, which annoys Them as They seem to go for all this stuff, though ' 'hin'. They're very anxiety-prone and jumpy every time this phone bell rings.

They're a funny couple. I love them, I really do. And when my arm plays up they give it a good rub. Their minds seem always to be racing about. He's always, but always, learning these things called lines, which She hears. He's been talking in Yorkshire quite recently so I understand every word. I'm not particularly impressed, but They laugh a lot.

Sometimes They leave me in this kitchen for as long as eight hours, and then tell me how good I have been. What They don't know is that I've eaten up all their aprons and torn them to shreds as a diversion. I don't mind being left in the kitchen. What I don't like so much is when They go to America or somewhere. It's all right now because I stay with Elizabeth and Tina and the kids and I enjoy it. As a matter of fact I enjoyed staying with these first people called Mr and Mrs Punter. He was very sweet. There were loads of other dogs there and he used to sit us up at the breakfast table and we all had cornflakes. That was before Elizabeth came to us.

There was one horrific occasion, though, when I seemed to get the idea that They thought maybe it would be better, as

They were away a great deal, if I stayed forever with these
Punters. I understood from this German sausage dog that there
was some man who wanted me. Well, I went there. Nice people.
Put me in front of the fire. But I felt my heart would break if I
never saw Them again. I thought of running away, but didn't
know where I was. I had a terrible acid stomach and was sure
I had a duodenal ulcer. I heard them talking and it appeared
that She had asked for me back as He was so depressed without
me.

Anyway, a surprise was arranged and dear Mrs Punter came
and took me away, back to my lovely home. It was arranged for
her to walk me past the magnolias and, when She gave the
signal, I was to be let loose. Well! I just raced into the library
and landed on His lap. Know what he did? He cried. Wasn't
that something? Really cried! And everyone had a drink and a
nut and *everybody* was happy. I've never seen tears on His face
before or since. She's different. She seems to cry at a drop of
a dog's biscuit. 'Oh,' He says, 'She's very emotional.' I think
She's a bit of a weirdo. She cries when trees are cut down
because they're dead anyway. She cries about People, Animals,
Birds, even when She reads Her own books! Once, when I
really stared at Her, She said: 'I can't help it, Chippo.' (She
calls me Chippo.) 'And, anyway, if I didn't cry at the sad parts
no one else would, and they're supposed to.'

Watching Her, I don't think She's mad about women, and
though She has quite a few girl friends, as She calls them, who
come in and out of the house, She definitely likes men best.

I think She's going blind. Just a hunch, of course. Mean to
say, when She's painting, She mumbles on to me about how
Renoir (whoever he is) saw everything through a blur, and if
that was good enough for him it's good enough for Her.

Somebody once asked Her if there was anything She was
frightened of, and She said, 'Yes, the disposal unit.' And I know
that's true: I've seen Her go purple in the face with rage when it
goes wrong and She has to put Her hand down this hole. She
has to, you see, because Her's is the smallest hand in the house,
except for mine, and mercifully no one has asked me to go near

the thing. She laughs a lot and so does He; They go off into these roars of laughter even when His big towel fell into the loo.

He's not a bit complex. I think He's probably the most wonderful chap I shall ever meet. He never loses his temper, even when, once, a taxi chopped the top of His finger off! He's always, but always, hurting his 'flippers' as She calls them, which means His hands. She calls them flippers because He's what's known as a Pisces, which means He's really a fish and should be swimming about in the sea. She calls Herself an Aquarius – that's someone who just sits on the bank of the river holding a pot full of water, or so She tells me. She lives on a sort of rainbow: She says she hears a 'distant drummer'. I never have heard one.

Sometimes She seems a million miles away, and has this far-away look in Her eyes as if they held some magic.

'Where's the magic gone?' She'll ask sometimes. I don't know what She's talking about, but He does. He's so gentle and understanding and kind to just anyone, He doesn't like rows and, if one is going on, He disappears. I really love this man and I follow Him everywhere. I'd rather be with Him than Her, because She says such odd things I don't understand, though I can understand what He's thinking.

She's keen on these Stars. She tells me I'm Gemini, which means She doesn't know which one of me is coming down the garden path. I'm keen on that idea.

He really takes care of Her. He does their breakfast on this Teasmade thing, lets me out for a leak, opens the shutters and brings up the papers They read. Then He gives Her a load of what they call vitamin pills, then He does His exercises, has a bath, listens to the news on this odd box, dresses – He's always neat and tidy, changes his knickers every day, and his socks. I know, because I watch Him from the chair. Meanwhile, She's in Her bath, where She washes Her undies in with Her. She talks to Herself a lot and sometimes She sneezes. I've heard Her sneeze about forty times. She has something called Asthma, whatever it is. I like licking her wet arms. Once, She was writing something in this bath. She said She hoped it would

make Her rise again after years of being submerged below the
waterline of a rusty old abandoned tanker: 'On the other hand,'
she said, 'I may very possibly only be a whitened corpse to be
eaten by the gulls.' I really don't know what She was talking
about.

Very often, He sits on this Wheel Horse with no head and cuts
the grass, while She roams around with this thing called a metal
detector. She's found some good bits of old money in the
garden. Once we went into the graveyard together and a big
man came up to Her. I went for his trousers, which didn't help.

'Anything you find here belongs to the dead,' he said, 'which
means the Rector.'

'I know,' She said.

'And I think it's disgusting the way this animal keeps lifting
'is leg on them gravestones.'

'He doesn't know it's a graveyard,' She said.

'Well, he does now,' he replied, and let fly at me with a huge
lump of turf that nearly blinded me.

They're always losing things, especially glasses and keys. I
have to retire sometimes to Disgrace Corner to keep my sanity.
They fumble through every coat and suit in the house, and
sometimes turn the whole place upside-down. I can only close
my eyes and hope it will soon be over. My idea of total boredom
is when one of Them says, 'Have you seen my reading glasses?'

One day, I found this rat-like thing and worried it all over the
garden. It turned out to be Her fur hat. I expected Her to be
furious, but She said She only used it for funerals.

3 Chips off the Block

THERE ARE THESE Grand Sons who belong to Them. The Chinese Empress Mimi says they're not really Grand at all, not to her way of thinking, which is of course Chinese. There are four of them, but only two live in England. The biggest is Crispian, the smallest is called Ace. They have a beautiful Mother called Hayley, and a tall father called Leigh, who has the whitest teeth I ever saw. Hayley is also called the Second Daughter. The First Daughter is called Juliet. She lives somewhere in a place called America and she has Sean and this Grand Daughter called Melissa. Then there's the Big Son called Jonathan, who has the third Grand Son called Henry; they don't live here either. It's all very confusing, but I've got the hang of it now.

Ace is not much bigger than me. I think he's the first human baby that I remember seeing. When I first saw him I laughed. My legs were as long as his trousers, and he had the littlest shoes I've ever seen. He runs everywhere at a great speed, often carrying a paper bag with goodies in it that people have given him. He has his own language, but we can understand each other. Once I asked him what he had in his paper bag.

'Nose drops,' he said, and put his hand over the opening of the paper bag. 'You'd better keep away from me. I've got Chicken Pox.'

'What's that?' I asked. *Chicken* Pox!

'It's spots all over ... you have to gargle,' he said.

'Gargle?' All this was new to me.

He looked at me and then surreptitiously took out what I afterwards learned was a ruler, something that all human children seem to carry. He gave me a whack across my bum.

'You're uneducated, so I have to smack you,' he said, and did it again.

I yelped. It hurt.

'Aaah,' She said. 'You mustn't hurt poor Chips.'

Ace got behind the sofa and squeezed my behind. Then he laughed, and climbed on to the sofa. He looks like a sort of cherub, but of course he's not. I decided to cut him dead and bide my time.

'He'll bite you, Ace darling, if you hurt him,' He said.

Not half I won't, and my teeth are as good as Fred the squirrel's. Ace sat on this sofa and they gave him a bottle of Coca Cola to keep him steady.

I edged up. 'Coca Cola', I said loftily, 'is *very* bad for your teeth.'

He paused in mid gulp and stared down at me.

'Look at Chippy! He wants to make friends with you, Ace. He wants a sip of your Coca Cola!' said his mother, Hayley.

Ace stared at me, and I stared at Ace. He offered me this straw, but I turned away.

'My friend at the Poodle Parlour where I get my hair cut', I said steadily, 'had this person called a Granny, and she was always being asked to take her teeth out by her Grand Sons...'

'Yes?' He queried nervously. 'Go on.'

'Drink up,' I said. 'Then I'll tell you.'

He drank the whole bottle.

'These Grand Sons', I said, 'put this Granny's teeth in a cup of Coca Cola.'

He stared at me.

I leaned against the sofa and looked idly round the room.

Everyone was having a good time, laughing and talking. They weren't concerned with Ace and me.

'Go on!' he shouted.

'When this Granny wanted her teeth back to eat with, the Grand Sons went back to this bowl ...'

'And?'

'... they had disappeared – been eaten up by this Coca Cola.'

He shrieked in horror and clapped his hand to his mouth.

'What *is* it, darling?' his beautiful mother asked.

He threw the empty bottle at me and fled out of the room with his mother running after him.

'Tit for tat,' I said to myself, and sprawled on Their rug.

The other Grand Son, Crispian, is bigger than me. Pretty soon he'll be too big to understand my language, because that's what happens when people get to a certain size, they forget. They're too high off the ground. They get too interested in things higher than the sofa. That's why He and She don't understand my language. Sometimes he's called Crispie

Noodles. Don't ask me why. He sat on this Poof thing and laughed; and after Ace had fled he opened his mouth very wide and bared all his teeth like an Alsatian.

'It's true,' I said.

'Well, I've been drinking Coca Cola since I was a few months old,' he said, and bared his teeth again.

'It's true,' I said again.

'Where did these teeth go to then, the granny's?' he asked.

'This Coca Cola disintegrated them,' I replied.

'What does that mean?'

'I don't know; I think it means made them disappear. The Coca Cola ate them up.'

'Well, my teeth are all right,' he retorted.

'That one in front is going a bad colour already.'

'That was a cricket ball, idiot!' he said wearily.

'That's what you think,' replied I knowingly.

His eyes widened. He got up and tried to look in the mirror, thereby nearly falling into the fire and getting a good slap from his beautiful mother Hayley. He was sent out of the room. He slashed at me with a ruler as he passed.

The Big Son has been here. He doesn't look like the others: he's a mixture of Him and Her, but tall and thin with dark red hair. He's very gentle and laughs a lot, too. He lives in America over this big pond called the Atlantic. They call him an adventurer; She calls him Hadji, which She says means traveller. He's not an actor. He says he isn't doing what he would like to do, because he would like to climb every mountain and go up and down all the dangerous rivers. I like listening to him talk, because he's been mostly everywhere, except China where She was born, and She says he's the only person she'd like to go on an adventure with except, of course, Him. Deep down, She's really an adventurer too, and sometimes in this kitchen She flings a pot on the floor, because She hates what She calls 'domesticity' and just wants to go off with a sleeping-bag, whatever that is. I do know the Big Son has one, because I've seen it in his room.

There is this other Grand Son, Henry, who is Big Son's son. He lives in America too, and eats these hamburgers. I bet he has a ruler somewhere. He has white hair and says 'sure' all the time. He's about the same size as Crispian. Sometimes he looks sad; I think it's because he has no mother. He's very sharp, too sharp for my liking: he'd hardly been here at all before he was sitting on the kitchen table eating chewing-gum and staring at me. Then he pointed at me and said very slowly in his American voice, 'That guy needs a trip to the dentist.'

'What do you mean darling?' She asked.

'I've been watching him eat. His teeth are covered in nicotine like he'd been smoking eight cigars a day.'

'He doesn't smoke, darling,' She said rather stiffly. 'Though I'll admit he does eat in rather a dirty way with his mouth wide open.'

I gave him a look and bit his ankle on my way out, moving quickly when he yelled.

The other day the other Grand Daughter arrived with her equally beautiful mother Juliet. This Grand Daughter's called Melissa. I must say They have beautiful children: all slim as sardines and wearing white hair. They talk a great deal and laugh very loudly all the time. Sometimes the din is so awful that I have to retire to Disgrace Corner or go up into His study, where there's a really comfy chair which sort of encloses you. Anyway, I like sitting on His trousers, especially when He's just had them in the presser because they're so warm. He doesn't care for it much, especially if it's His evening dress trousers, though as I told you I don't moult, so I don't know what He's on about.

Juliet has a son, too, called Sean. No one seems to see him much apart from his beautiful mother – I never have anyway. He seems to spend a great deal of time in what they call surf; he's a champion surfer, which might have something to do with a washing machine.

Crispian is what They call accident prone: he only has to turn his head suddenly and hit the door knob, and he knocks himself

out. Once he even bit off half his tongue, which I could have
told him was not a good idea.

This Melissa interests me. She's three years old now. The last
time she was here, she was a baby in a thing called a cot, which
is really a type of dog basket with wooden sides so that she can't
fall out. Mind you, this Ace gets out of anything, even the
barrier they put across the stairs. He got over it like a cat and
fell into what they called a valuable bowl of flowers, which he
broke of course.

'Oh well,' She said. 'Come easy, come go.' But then Her
Brother the Captain mended it anyway, so I never knew what
all the caterwauling was about.

Another thing about this Melissa, even though she's only
three she really talks. Not only to me of course, but when she
talks to the Humans, she's really bright; she has her own kind of
voice.

'Gude monning,' she says, and 'Deesy chins', but they all
understand her. Now, when Ace talks to Humans he has a type
of Italian waiter's voice.

'I donta wanta goa,' he says. 'Mea noa lika puddinga.' He's
very quick is Ace, he could end up a genius. His eyes, when he
looks at you, are always half closed, as if he was going to whack
you with something, in my case with this ruler.

Crispian is really clever, he knows the answer to practically
everything, and he draws well. He's going to be an actor he told
me once when we were jogging along on this Wheel Horse with
no head.

'I asked Him who His agent was, and He told me, so I rang
up and the chap is taking care of it,' he told me.

'Taking care of what?' I asked, nearly strangled by his hand.

'My career, of course. We've all got to have one.'

'Of course.'

'What's yours, Chips?'

'Well ... well ... mean to say. I'm the guard round here. I
sound off when the bell rings ... and other things ...'

'Not enough.' He shook his head sadly. 'Haven't you any
ambition?'

I wanted to get off this wretched Horse. I didn't know what to say.

'I'd like to fly,' I said.

'*That* is ridiculous,' he answered.

I got off the miserable thing, and took a leak on the apple tree for comfort.

'It's Melissa's birthday today,' he shouted as he drove away. 'She's going to give her a Koala Bear that sings.'

I sat down and had a good scratch. I felt very ignorant suddenly, a Bear that sings! – what next? I'd never seen a Bear anyway; how big would it be? I got the horrors, especially as I knew the house was going to be full of Cousins and things, mostly boys with rulers and probably girls with knitting needles.

I saw Melissa coming towards me all dressed up with His stalking hat on her head. I also saw Fred. They'll have to watch out for Fred you know, he's getting pretty savage. I think he's hungry, but then he's a bit of a twerp. Why doesn't he eat all those nuts instead of burying them and then forgetting where he put them? I watched him, ready to chase in case he hurt her.

'Darling Melissa baby,' She called. 'What are you trailing along behind you into the orchard?'

'Lavvy paper,' Melissa answered.

'I wonder why?' She asked.

'Like to,' was the answer. 'So yew can find me when I gets lorst.'

Ace, I noticed, was gathering it up from the other end, and suddenly all the roses were awash with this stuff; finally it got tangled up in this Horse and He had to come out and dislodge it. He was quite angry – for Him.

'Go inside and get ready for the party!' He shouted. And they did.

Fred and I looked at each other.

I wondered what lavvy paper was anyway, mean to say, what was the purpose of it?

I took a stroll when they'd all gone. I keep out of these party arrangements. Not that I could help. He and She get into such a *thing* about it. He washes away at endless glasses; she has all these things called Jellies all over the kitchen table; somebody fixes candles (just the three); the whole room is crammed with people laughing and talking and walking about with knives and things, sandwiches and other bits of food.

I looked at my empty plate.

'Poor Chippo,' She said. 'You'll have to waity waity, won't you?'

I went out and studied the general situation. I noticed that the Koo Koos have jumped the gun. They're rebuilding their nest outside His bathroom window. Don't they *know* it's much too early? We could have snow, black frost or a hurricane! Then they'd be blown all over the joint, smashing their eggs, their legs, even their wings. Then I know what will happen: She'll bring them into the library and feed them, put them on a radiator or something wrapped in stuff called Kleenex, and stick them in a cigar box with a doll's hot-water bottle at nights. I know, I've seen Her do it to a linnet who was egg bound. That was a pitiful experience.

I remember once old Harold found a Redwing in the orchard – it's a kind of thrush but more beautiful – it had really been lacerated by a cat or some other animal. I remember Ace and Crispian were here then, and they all did their best, but this fellow died; he was too far gone. So we had a burial. Crispian was the grave-digger, because he said he had had a lot of experience as he was forever burying these mice that their cat got hold of. Ace was the Chief Mourner.

We took this long, mournful pace past the vegetable garden and Crispian excavated this dicey hole by the cold frame and, after hours of mumbling, Ace stuck this Redwing in the hole wrapped up in a dishcloth. Then they mumbled some more and threw a lot of gravel at the poor thing, pushed the earth back on, and erected a huge cross, with REDWING written on it with Her lipstick. Afterwards, we all went back to the library for tea and snakes and ladders. What an idiotic game!

I often think of the Redwing when I go by, so this time I took a leak on this cross to show I remember.

I meandered round the garden while they got on with their arrangements. Harold was at this bonfire as usual. He looked up when he saw me and muttered something. I drew closer.

'I could swear I heard someone call out Harold,' he said. We both looked round; there was no sign of anyone. He looked over the hedge into this potato field. No one. He called out to Sam, the next door gardener.

'Hear anything like a call, Sam?' he asked. The other man shook his head.

Now, I can tell you, there *is* something in this garden, and in the house too. A quiet, gentle whispering voice. I've often heard it and barked, specially down by this bonfire where I go every night and really yell. Once, I even saw something white that you could see through. It really scared me, because I could see through it to the Norwegian Spruce.

They all think it's a white cat, but I know better. They explain it all away by saying old Harold is a Celt like She is, and they see things. But, as I heard Her say once, 'It stands to reason that a house and garden over four hundred years old must have something remaining of all those years. Things still planted in the air.' She may be a Celt, whatever that is, but She believes there are other people here from all those years ago, and so do I, so maybe I'm a Celt too.

I wandered back to Melissa's party. Melissa's birthday party – what a hoot! They get this chap called Smarty Artie Crafty to amuse the kids while all the grown-up Humans gobble up the tea. He seems as thick as two planks to me, but they all fall about and scream with mad laughter. I knew it would turn me on and I'd go for his trousers, which is exactly what I did. He was dressed as some sort of clown and I just couldn't take it. There was the general disorder of bursting balloons, squeals and shouts, and the next thing I knew I was in Disgrace Corner with the door shut.

I may add, my birthday came and went and nobody, but nobody did a thing about it. I was pretty cheesed off. They were all having a whale of a time in there, and I was only trying to join in the fun and bite a few balloons. Admittedly, I went for Smarty Artie Crafty's trousers, but so what? The Grand Children thought it was funny, though of course *he* didn't, but he didn't complain.

I wished I'd been put in the kitchen. At least in there I could have bitten off all the apron strings.

She came in.

'Why are you such a destructive naughty boy?' She asked.

I put my feet up on the wall and didn't answer.

'Well,' She said. 'You can go out in the garden.'

She opened the door. I looked into the hall where they were having so much fun.

'Go on,' She said. 'Out in the garden and go and find a white pussy cat to chase.' Pussy cat! She knows there are hardly any pussy cats! She sees to that because of the Birds. Mean to say, if

She does see a cat, She throws something after it, and it flies for its life.

She closed the door and I was left staring at nothing. Suddenly I got an idea to put things right: I'd dig up my old lamb bone and bring it in. I found it under the Sweet Peas and brought it into the kitchen. It was huge, but I managed it by walking steadily.

No one noticed me, they were too busy with these nasty jellies and sandwiches, so I took it up to the spare room where an Important Person was going to sleep and I put it under her pillow. I knew on which side of this gigantic bed She'd sleep, because that's where you turn on this fire that makes the bed warm. Then I went downstairs and sat in a corner watching them all make fools of themselves, but I didn't join in any more. I was too clever.

That night there was murder. The Important Person shrieked when my lovely present was discovered, though She and He fell about with laughter.

It's difficult to win.

4 Home Defence

I'VE JUST BEEN talking to Mimi. She takes a leak sitting down. They're always trying to guide her to the gravel path, as she leaves her own particular mark on the velvet lawn.

She's not feeling too good, she told me. She hasn't recovered from the incident which happened the other night when They went to London. There were just the three of us: Melodie, Mimi and Yours Truly. Melodie was in the bath, and Mimi and I were minding our own business with her fish whiskers. Suddenly, this insane bell went off in our ears.

'It's him!' I screamed.

'It's who?' Mimi asked calmly.

'The monster shut in the broom cupboard,' I yelled.

'Why does he ring a bell?' she asked. It was ringing like a maniac.

'It means he knows They've gone and he wants to get out,' I told her.

'Let him get out if he can,' was all she said.

'No, no, no. You don't understand. We must find Melodie, she's big enough to hit him with the hoover.'

We went to the bathroom. Melodie was scared too. I could see that. She was wallowing about in this water.

'Oh boy, what a fright,' said Melodie and grabbed her bath-robe.

The front doorbell started ringing.

'He's got out! He's got out!' I wailed.

'Pull yourself together,' snapped the Empress. 'You're the only man in the house and you're behaving like a silly mouse.'

That steadied me a bit. We followed Melodie, dripping wet, down to the hall, and she opened the door. There were these two policemen standing there.

'Your burglar alarm has gone off,' one of them said.

'I know,' she bleated. 'I don't know why.'

'I think we'd better come in and have a good look round,' the other man said.

'Oh, please do,' begged Melodie. 'Go everywhere, the cupboards, the shelves, under the beds ...'

'Now, keep quite calm, dear,' they said. 'We're here.'

They came in and I went for their trousers and ankles, but I was really going for them. They kicked out at me.

'Chips!' she shouted nervously.

'Chips!' shouted Mimi in a voice I've *never* heard before. 'Hang on like grim death even if they kick you in the teeth.' Which is what they were doing. 'I don't believe they're policemen at all!' she said in her high, sing-song voice.

Whereupon, to my astonishment, she got hold of the leg of the other chap.

'Thought you hadn't any teeth!' I said.

'I have when I want to use them,' she said. I really have to hand it to her. After all, she's a hundred years old, but to see her clinging to this lad's trousers you'd think she was still in Shangri La. Melodie's towel coat was all over the place. She was decent, of course, but it was a struggle, I could see that.

'My Gawd!' they said. 'Anyone would think they were a couple of Alsatians. They won't let go, and we can't move.'

This monster was still screaming from the cupboard.

'It's bedlam, that's what it is,' one of them said.

Melodie got hold of us, but we still hung on. Their trousers were up to their knees and they looked downright stupid. I was panting – I thought I'd caught Her asthma – when this nice girl from across the road appeared. She's called Nem, and she has these big dogs that always get the marrow bones I'm not allowed to have.

'Miss,' these two policemen said, 'we can't move because these two tigers have got us in a half Nelson. Wish we had our sniffer dogs with us.' I knew what they meant – those Alsatians who would have mangled us!

'Where is it?' Nem asked. 'I'll turn it off.'

Melodie was in a right state. She leaned against the table with her mouth open.

'Broom cupboard,' she whispered.

This Nem went off and obviously bashed the heck out of the monster, because he stopped shrieking. By this time, these two men were out in the road with Mimi and I still hanging on to their trousers.

'They'll be killed by a car!' Melodie moaned.

'Jolly good thing if they are,' they said. This Nem got hold of us both.

'Let go you twerps,' she said. 'They really are policemen.' We let go. They were pretty angry.

'You don't need a burglar alarm with this lot,' they said, and got into their car with the blue light and drove away.

When They came home Melodie told Them about it.

'Poor Melodie,' He said. 'I expect Mr Chips and Mimi didn't see the blue light on the police car.'

Next day They thought we were both ill. Mean to say, we were. It took us a couple of days to recover. One of my teeth was even loose. Mimi just slept on her cushion for so long that I thought she was dead, and we'd have another funeral by the greenhouse.

'That was bad,' I said to her.

'Bad,' she said, 'but not impossible.' And she went to sleep again.

It's rather funny, because Melodie keeps saying how skittish Mimi has become. We wander all over the garden together and laugh like mad. Where I leak, she leaks. She seems much more active and amused about everything, particularly about the white bread She feeds these silly birds. Mimi says it has to be very constipating, but they all eat it hurriedly and noisily without thinking.

Yes, Mimi and I have really got everything together, and we have a ball. No one quite knows why Mimi has taken this turn for the better.

But I know!

Melodie says she'd better go back to her mother for a while, in case ... In case of what, I should like to know! She's coming for a picnic tomorrow and taking Mimi home. I heard Melodie and Her talking.

'She *is* a hundred,' Melodie said. 'It could kill her. And anyway what would they be? Pekinyorkshires, or Yorkshire Pekinese, or just Pekeyorks, or Yorkypekes?'

'Might be a new breed,' She said.

What a swizz the whole thing is, I thought.

Well, she *did* go away. 'Just for a long weekend,' They said in comforting tones.

I couldn't believe she'd gone. I kept going up to her suite, waiting outside the door, calling 'Mimi' quietly. Melodie let me in, and I had a good scrounge around. She certainly wasn't there. There were woolly bears and dogs and all the things Melodie goes to bed with, but no sign anywhere of my friend Mimi.

'He's pining,' She said.

'Hide your furry boots,' replied Melodie. I do not know what they were all talking about.

I was sad when Mimi went, because for one thing *everyone* else seemed to go too. There was a lot of packing and shouting as usual, and laughs about airplane tickets, and cars coming and taking them all away, and suddenly there was a horrible silence all over the house, and He and She got stuck into their rooms and started reading things called Scripts, and the phone voice drooled on about 'arrangements', and I can tell you I began to get really nervous, even though Margaret and Elizabeth came and shoved this hoover about and went away, and we all ate our food and looked at this ghastly thing called television again.

'You'll like the telly soon, Chips', She said one day, 'because He'll be on it!'

How could He suddenly be on this box? It's too small for a start. Mean to say, how can He suddenly climb into this thing and still be in the room with us?

'And you can come on location and run about in the fields and chase things like rabbits under the hedges,' She told me.

Mind you, I have to say that I like this telly on Saturdays. I really do. I'm mad for the All Blacks. They look like animals, all crunched up together and rolling on the ground. I don't understand what they're up to, but I get excited when they tear all over the place. Then I like this Welsh singing and flags and that. I watch that. I like racing too, all these idiotic but lovely horses going like mad at these hedges. She keeps on phoning someone called Mr Hill about this scrimmage, don't ask me why. Then comes this thing called Boxing. I can't take that, all that sniffling and blood, but for some reason He really goes for that. I think it's hideous to watch two Humans beating the hell out of each other and people yelling. I suppose if it was two lions I wouldn't mind, but Humans! To start with, they look so silly whacking away at each other on a sort of plate.

I was confused. Totally confused. I had to get away and think, so one day, when the lych-gate was open and no one was looking, I slipped out into this graveyard next door. I love this place, it's so mysterious and so quiet. Humans only come in sometimes carrying flowers, and they lay them on these weird stones which say 'In Loving Memory', or they plant little things, and kneel down and mutter something, and then they go away. Sometimes they wipe their eyes too as if something was in them.

I was having a ball, frolicking about, digging, leaking and generally enjoying myself. The church door was open and I even went in and had a good look round all these seats which were great to leak on. The Rector was there dressed up as a ghost in this long white thing he wears, and he drove me off with some broom he had in his hand.

'Why can't dogs go to church?' I barked at him.

He just shouted 'Clear off!', so I had to, though I gave him a bit of a run as I got as far as the steps to the altar.

I went back to this graveyard. I was panting a bit so I lay down on one of these stones which said 'In Loving Memory' and thought why shouldn't dogs go to church? Why shouldn't sheep, or cows, or horses? Mean to say, even Fred has the right to get in there if there was anything he wanted to eat or drink! Mean to say, there's a thing called a Font full of water; birds

would like that in the cold weather when everything is iced up, even though She breaks the bird-bath up with a hammer. It didn't make sense to me. After all, someone must have made us all, and if this is a special house, anyone should be able to go in there, *anyone*. I bet the mice get in there. These humans are forever tolling away with these noisy bells, and I always understood it was to call people in for some reason or other. So, why not animals and birds as well as these humans in hats?

I lay on my back in the sun. It was warm, not raining for once, and I was really happy – especially after last night.

Although we live next to this church, Him and Her don't go in
too often when these noisy bells are ringing and, when they do,
They never take me. Why? I ask myself. I can go to pubs and
restaurants, Gerrards Cross, the Golf Course, but not this
church.

Once, I heard Her say She didn't go as much to this place as
She would like, because of this First, Second and Third series,
whatever that means!

'I don't want to be told to shake hands with total strangers,'
She said. 'I want to go in there and pray, and think quietly
about one of my plays that nobody wants, and sing all the old
hymns I knew as a child with the old chants, I *don't* want to find
myself in there with twenty squalling babies all being christ-
ened out of a salad bowl.' He laughed and agreed. Now, I'm
only repeating Her words, I am not going to try and explain any
of it because I don't understand a single word. I just happen to
have good recall of conversations. Talking of conversations,
this one exhausted me. I hardly slept. I suppose it was a row –
but it went like this:

SHE: I can't breathe. That is to say, I can't really get a big
     breath.
HE: Why not?
SHE: I ate too much, and it was your fault for having grilled
     mackerel.
HE: You stuffed all this rice.
SHE: I was hungry. But feel my stomach, it's like a balloon and if
     you eat or drink too much liquid, it sits on the bottom part of
     your lung and you get asthma ... you don't answer, are you
     asleep?
HE: No.
SHE: Well, why are you snoring?
HE: I'm not, I'm not asleep. Oh my back! Can you put some
     Deep Heat on it?
SHE: Here I am, unable to breathe, and all you can think about
     is your back. I'll kiss you goodnight, in case I'm dead in the
     morning.

HE: Goodnight, darling.

I was restive. I didn't like all this talk so I jumped on the bed.

SHE: Basket, Chips.

That means go to bed, so I kissed Them all round and went back to this sofa.

HE: I think you've knocked your water over.
SHE: I have.

She put the light on and mopped up while He groaned.

SHE: Well I've got to see haven't I! Oh I do hope my prescription for this special chewing gum comes soon, it's supposed to make you stop smoking.
HE: You smoke too much, especially when you're writing.
SHE: I'm going to stop, and I'll never eat mackerel again.

They seemed to sleep after that, but I couldn't.

5 On Location

WELL, HE STARTED this television film. It was something called *The Quiet Ass*, I think. He had a lot of white hair and whiskers all over Him. I didn't like to look, because He's not really like that. He had some awful-looking clothes on him, too. He was surrounded by Humans of all sorts like the All Blacks rugger scrum; wherever He went they all had to follow. It didn't seem to bother Her. We were in this caravan thing, and She just kept on making tea or writing things down on some book. She asked me if I wanted to go O, U, T – which means out. I said I did, and she opened the door and I fell on to the grass.

Well, there must have been a hundred thousand people there! Huge lamps and cameras and endless other cars. These Humans were all over Him, like wasps. Now and again, some chap would say 'Good little doggie', but when I went for their ankles they soon left me alone, except for one who kicked me! Boy, did I hang on to *his* trousers. This chap let out such a yelping and caterwauling that He had to come over and smooth things down and put me back into this caravan thing with Her. She didn't seem to care one way or the other. Although it was terribly cold in there, She didn't seem to notice. She was too busy.

I wandered off again. Freedom. Everybody was concerned with lights, megaphones, cameras and shouting. I was alone and loved every minute of it. The hedgerows were full of things that moved suddenly, then stopped. I had a good burrow about even though my hair was torn out by these brambles.

It was getting darker now, and I looked back to see which way I had come. To my horror I could see nothing as this mist had come down between them and me. Suddenly I was frightened. I wasn't sure which way to go. I could run along the hedgerow of course, but which way was I facing? This hedge had been on my left, I was sure of that, so I started running like mad. I could hear nothing and reckoned I must have gone further than I thought.

All of a sudden I came face to face with this figure. It was a dog, no doubt about that, but not one I'd ever seen, and against the darkening sky he looked a bit terrifying.

He made a run at me which I evaded, I don't know how, as I was frozen with terror. I started running again, but his long thin legs soon outstripped me, and again he faced me. He had a great many teeth which shone in the twilight. I sat down and stared him in the face.

'Sucker,' he said.

'I'm not a sucker,' I replied, as casually as I could.

'What are you then?'

'I'm a Yorkshire terrier.'

He laughed. 'Lucky I didn't get you by the scruff of that neck and throw you over the hedge,' he said. 'Because I could have. Or I could just have eaten you. You'd make a good mouthful for a hungry Whippet.'

'It wouldn't have been as easy as that,' I replied, lofty-like. 'I've got very strong teeth and could have done you a nasty injury where it hurts most.'

He laughed again. 'What are you doing here anyway?'

'Minding my own business. As a matter of fact, I'm filming.'

'Oh, you're filming, are you!'

'I just came here for a look round, and now I seem to be lost. Is this ... is it your garden?'

'Everywhere is my garden if that's what you call a field. I'm a hunter, you see.'

'I see.'

Another figure loomed into sight. Another big dog, just as strange looking, except that his eyes were sad.

'We're both hunters, and you're the hunted!'

I knew I was at a disadvantage with these two, and looked nervously over my shoulder at the gathering gloom.

'This sucker is lost,' this Whippet said to the other dog.

'I won't do you any harm if you'd be kind enough to tell me where all those cars and things are,' I said brightly.

'He won't do us any harm! – this miserable water-rat won't do *us* any harm!'

'Water-rat ... WATER-RAT!' I shouted. 'I bet I can run as fast as either of you!'

'Possibly. Water-rats can run fast too.'

I pushed past them and started running, I ran the fastest I have ever run, in the direction I hoped I had come from. They ran slowly beside me, loping along easy-like. All of a sudden, they'd disappeared, but only for a second, then they came back.

'See?'

I saw ...

'Look,' I said. 'If you'll show me the way back to all those cars and things, I'll see you get a good meal, I will really.'

'All those cars and things have gone,' said this Whippet.

'Gone? They couldn't have gone without me!'

The mist was getting thicker. I was getting more scared. What to do, what to do?

'That's what they've done, Rat.'

The other dog spoke for the first time. 'Better come back to our place. Have some hedgehog soup.'

'Sounds revolting,' I replied.

They turned away and after a second I followed them. It was the only thing to do. On the way I asked them their names.

'Mine is Wellington, for no good reason,' replied the Whippet, 'and he's called Barmy. He's a Lurcher.'

'I see,' I answered. 'I'm called Chips.'

'Oh,' they both said.

We came at last to the strangest place. There were about five houses on wheels, and it was really filthy. Well, I've seen cars!

bright shining cars, but these were all mangled and squashed, like they'd been in a gigantic accident; mud and hoards of fearsome and dirty-looking children, dirty garbage and paper everywhere.

'What sort of place is this?' I asked.

'It's where the gyppos live,' replied Barmy.

A fat woman came out of one of the houses on wheels. She looked at me, and I looked at her.

''E got nice eyes, but I don't think 'e's pedigree.'

'Sort of wonk,' said someone else. 'Might be good watchdog. What shall we call 'im?'

'Redford,' she said.

'Redford? What does that mean anyways?'

'Puts me in mind of Robert Redford. Got the same 'air-do.'

Who the heck Robert Redford was I did not know, nor did I care.

'Better give 'im a drop to eat, settle 'im down. 'Ere, give 'im some bread and milk.'

I stared at the bread and milk. I thought of Mimi and constipation. I turned away, even though I was starving. I would have given anything for a bowl of water. My tongue was sticking to the roof of my mouth.

A troop of kids came along. They didn't have rulers or nose-drops. One of them cuddled me and offered me some chewing-gum. I turned that down too. I wasn't going to eat anything – like a prisoner of war.

They put a heavy chain on me and tied me under this house on wheels. I heard them talking above me.

'What you going to do if 'e don't 'ave nothing on his collar, no tag like?' I thanked my stars I didn't have M.C.P. First Class.

Barmy and Wellington sat beside me under this house.

'Would you like a cigarette?' Wellington asked.

'Cigarette? I've never smoked in my life!'

'I eat the fag ends,' he said. 'Stops you being hungry.'

What a different world, I thought. They looked so dirty.

'When did you two have a bath?' I asked.

'What's a bath?' asked Barmy.

What's a bath! Here am I fighting against getting into His bath and then feeling great and everyone brushing me, and telling me how pretty I look, and these two guys didn't even know what a bath was! I really began to feel so sorry for these two deprived guys. This garbage was beginning to smell in the late sunset.

'Well,' I said, 'this is just about the worst thing that ever happened to me, but I'm not staying here. I'm getting out.'

'How? And where will you go if you can go?' asked Wellington.

I stared at the trees overhead. They were black and dangled dismally.

'I'm not in a position to say *yet*,' I replied, 'but I will get out.'

'Where will you go?'

'I have to admit I don't know, but I'll go on going till I get somewhere,' I replied.

'You'll be years at it, years!' Barmy said.

'Redford,' somebody shouted.

'That's you,' he said.

'R-e-d-f-o-r-d!' A small boy 'appeared with a bowl in his
hand. It smelled good. 'There's a good boyo,' this chap said,
and put it down beside me.

I was just about to have a taste when these two dogs went at it
like lunatics until it was all gone.

'That was for me!' I remonstrated.

'You wouldn't have liked it,' said Barmy, licking his lips. 'It
were hedgehog soup.'

'Frankly,' I said, 'I wouldn't have cared what it was. I'm so
hungry I would have eaten anything.'

'Oh, let's get some sleep, for Gawd's sake,' said Wellington.
'It'll be dawn soon and I want to be after these hares.'

We lay close together. My brain was working furiously.

'Would you two help me to get away?' I asked.

'I suppose we *could* cause a diversion.'

'At your own risk, don't forget.'

'And there would have to be something in it for us.'

The night seemed endless, and Barmy really smelt. He kept
on scratching.

'What are you doing?' I asked.

'Counting my teeth,' he said.

For something to do, I started counting mine, and somehow
it took my mind off things. Don't give up, I kept telling myself.
Wait for the right moment. Keep your eyes on the lads.

I fell asleep thinking of the Yorkshire Light Infantry.

6 Lost and Found

I REALLY DON'T know how long I was in this wretched place. It could have been days, weeks or months. I just know it was interminable.

'The kids, they like 'im,' said the big man. By now I knew he was called by the name of Ben.

I suppose they did like me. Well, I was different – different in every way from Wellington and Barmy who lived their own lives, going where they wanted to, lying about when they wanted to. They seemed contented enough with their lives, but I kept on remembering my lot, wherever they were. Them and Harold, Elizabeth, Margaret – the whole bulging household. Mind you, I wasn't given much time to cogitate. These kids dragged me all over this dirty area on my long chain. 'Come on, Redford! This way, Redford. Good boy, Redford.' I nearly went bananas, but I didn't have much choice.

I must have been bathed ten times, they thought it was a fun game. I wished they'd bathed themselves, they all smelled to high heaven. I was certain I was going to get pneumonia, and all these two jerks, Wellington and Barmy, did, was to laugh.

'When are you going to make this diversion?' I asked at night.

'When it's a good and proper time?' was all they said.

As for the food! Well, in the end I *had* to get on with hedgehog soup, but I got quite fond of these things called Mars bars, which they ate all day – the kids, I mean.

The old lady was quite decent. She dried me in some filthy old towel.

'Looks like a little old rat when 'e's wet, don't 'e?' she said, and they agreed. ' 'E amuses the kids, too and 'e don't eat much. 'E's a nice little thing; 'e'll get used to us soon and then 'e don't 'ave to be on the chain no more.'

I licked her outstretched hand. 'You're sweet, Redford,' she said, 'that's what you are.'

Strangely enough, they were all sweet in their way. They were all filthy dirty and full of lice, and the camp where we lived was really disgusting, like an enormous dustbin everywhere. They came into this house on wheels, and they were really nice to each other, sharing their food, ready to defend each other, and very poor. Sometimes the Police came by but they only looked into the houses on wheels and went away again.

'I'm lame,' Ben used to say. 'I'm just a crooked carcase.' And he spread his big arms against the red ceiling of the caravan. 'I'm just a scarecrow.' And he muttered and groaned in a corner with his bowl of hedgehog soup. I was sorry for this enormous man, I really was. Somehow, well, gyppos seem such lonely people. They don't have the same freedom as They do, as I was pretty soon to know ...

The Police cleared us off.

We were sent away to another place; it was under something called the M40. It became more dangerous there, with all these cars whirling round. Amazing really how quickly they made a real dump of it all – paper everywhere, and sometimes they lit a great fire, and all the faces were suddenly bright, strange faces – faces I had never seen before. But then my life had only been Jamboree and the Big Old House by the church in our village; here I was always on this old chain.

One night I asked Wellington when they were going to make this diversion they talked about.

'Aren't you settling down?' he asked.

'I certainly am not,' I replied. 'I want to get the hell out of here and back to my people.'

'You'll be surprised how soon these people will become your people,' he said.

'Not on your nelly,' I told him. 'Mind you, I like them, mucky as they are, but I'm here to tell you that once a Yorkshireman has given his allegiance to anyone, that is absolutely that.'

'I see,' he said.

'So ...'

'So what?' he asked.

'I have to get away, back to Them.'

'Oh,' he said.

'And to the flowers, the velvety lawn ...'

'We have flowers,' he said. 'Not here, of course, but there are places we go to where there's dandelion, cowslip, ragged robin pimpernel, poppy, bindweed ...'

'What do all these names mean? You're talking about common weeds – bindweed! Harold spends hours killing it. So does She. *I* mean those beautiful long things that grow in this herbaceous garden. Delphiniums. That's what he calls them.'

'Who does?'

'Harold, that's who.'

'Never heard of 'em,' said Barmy. 'But I just love bindweed and vetches, lady's smock and sow thistles.'

'Really?'

'Nobody has to do anything to them, you just lie in them in the sun. They grow round the caravan.'

'Phew! You mean all round this junk heap they cook up?'

'Nobody has to plant them, nobody. They're just there.'

'Delphiniums! What about foxgloves and cow parsley?' I asked.

'What about them?'

'I like them,' I said, thinking of Melissa.

'Okay, I'll give you them,' he said as he turned away and slouched off.

We kept on being pushed away. It seemed no one, but no one, liked Gypsies, and everywhere we went it was another junk heap and in a matter of days or minutes it was really disaster corner. This old chain was really beginning to get me down. It was so heavy; it pulled my head practically down to the ground. I spent most of my time sighing. Wellington and Barmy watched me from afar. I think they were sorry for me in their way, but old Ben with the bloodshot eyes never turned a hair.

These two guys, Wellington and Barmy, never missed a trick, they had their eyes on everything that was going on.

'Tomorrow,' said Wellington.

'Tomorrow what?' I asked.

'We'll put the mockers on them,' he said.

'Mockers?'

'See that black-haired boy over there?'

'Yes.'

'We seen 'im lookin' at your collar, see?'

'My collar?'

'Right. 'E wants your nice green collar for hisself.'

'Why?'

'Don't ask me. But we seen 'im starin' at it. And believe us 'e's gonna get it. 'E'll put it round 'is own neck.'

'What for?'

'Don't ask us. But when we see 'im take it orf of your neck we'll cause this diversion.'

'When will that be?'

'Could be any time. Probably at night.'

'At night ... What will you do, better let me in on it.'

'We'll cause an uproar in that hedge over there. Everyone'll rush out, and *you*, if you have any sense, will tear away.'

'Where to?'

'Anywhere, twerp. Just keep on going. They'll never see you in the dark.'

'North, South, East or West?'

'Anything that comes into your head. You're a terrier aren't you? Just keep going, it doesn't matter where. Then sit down and think.'

'Oh, my whiskers! I'll miss you two ...'

'You simply can't afford to be sentimental.'

'If only one of you could come with me ...' The soles of my feet started to sweat and go cold. Did I really want to go after all? Would They have forgotten me? Would I get into worse trouble? Would I ever find Them anyway?

'You've gone pale,' said Barmy.

'I feel a little sick,' I replied.

'The trouble with you pet dogs is, you're spoilt. You don't know the meaning of looking after yourselves, your owners sit you on a nice cushion and indulge you, don't they?' asked Wellington.

I thought of my basket with the sheepskin rug that moulted on their brown carpet, and said nothing.

'Wellington and I have had to fight for our last crust of bread, haven't we, Wellington?'

Wellington nodded.

'*You'll* find out between here and there that you don't know who to trust.'

I was taking it all in. I had a lump of misery in my throat.

'We have to fight for our freedom. They slam doors in your

face, give you a good kick, or they drag you into their shacks and you're a prisoner again.'

'P'raps I'll stay,' I said gloomily.

'No, no, you keep on saying you've got to get back to Them. Here's a chance to learn to stand up for yourself,' said Barmy.

'He's not very big,' said Wellington.

'Not easily caught either, we presume to hope,' replied Barmy.

'I certainly *can* run fast,' I answered, 'but where to?'

'We can at least see above the weeds,' Wellington said, scratching like hell.

'All the better, he's got the undergrowth to hide in.'

'Sounds as if you want to get rid of me,' I said sadly.

'Look here, you're forever asking us to make a diversion, and when we work it all out for you, you go chicken.'

'Chicken!'

'Sure, chicken. Means "scared" in case you never learned the word.'

It was getting darker. I glanced over my shoulder and saw the black-haired boy staring at me.

'See?' said Barmy. ''E wants yer collar.'

Some time later, when it was really dark and all the houses on wheels had their lights on, Barmy edged up to me.

'We're going to do it now ... 'e's coming over. Just sit casual like, let 'im take it, and when we start this uproar, scaper, jest scaper.'

'Scaper?'

'Go for your life through those fields and woods, and if you gets hungry, catch anything you see and eat it – something small I mean, like a mouse or a squirrel.'

'Squirrel!'

'Ah, 'e'd never catch one of them,' said Wellington.

'Before all this horror happens,' I said, 'I want to thank you both for your help. I hope ... I hope we'll meet again and I can do something for you two.'

I was nearly in tears. I was a prisoner escaping, and I was scared, chicken ...

' ''E's coming.'

The black-haired boy came up to me silently.

'There's a good little squirt,' he said, and unloosed my collar. I sat there, unmoving, like they told me to.

'Okay, Barmy,' said Wellington. 'Now!'

'Good luck, chum!' said Barmy, and they sped away across all this muck to the hedge and started barking and yelling.

At first my legs wouldn't move. I knew they had to. I didn't want to be despised by a whippet and a lurcher. I was free, but I wasn't myself.

The doors of the houses on wheels opened and the world seemed to be rushing to this hedge. I fled for my life, stumbling and falling over my lame leg which hurt like hell from all those days and nights in the open. I was panting and crying and carrying on alarmingly, but I did what they said, made for the fields and woods in the opposite direction, banging into trees and stumps. I heard a shot somewhere behind me and stopped. A hare heard it too, and he stopped in his tracks. He eyed me suspiciously. I stared at him; I'd never seen such huge ears.

'Go on the grass,' he said, 'so they can't hear the twigs cracking.' And then he'd gone. He looked a hundred years old.

I must have gone for miles. I was dead tired. There was a big house ahead of me with lights in all the windows, only it wasn't on wheels. It reminded me of *our* house. In front of me was a shed. The door was shut, so I crawled in under a hole in the netting. It was alive with these things called chickens! They set up such a caterwauling they scared the heck out of me, but I couldn't say anything as they were birds, and I don't speak 'bird'. I sat down beside one of them; it was on some kind of a nest, and no way was she going to move. Then, to my horror, some small yellow things came out from underneath her ... yellow and fluffy, with bird's legs. They crawled all over me. I closed my eyes and let them. This chicken sort of smiled at me with her eyes – at least, I thought it was a smile. There was something in a tin near her; I ate it up, I was so hungry. These other chickens had stopped their shrieking and started pecking around me. There was no sound now. I fell asleep.

I was woken up suddenly by these screaming birds, flapping and flying all round me, except the one beside me on the nest. Whatever it was she was holding her ground. I admired her guts. I looked around. Under the same hole that I had come in through was something digging like crazy. It was very dark; I couldn't see what it was. I thought of my chums.

'Wellington? Barmy? Is that you then?' The scrabbling and digging went on. These chicks were scared out of their lives, I could see that. Even the old bird beside me was all ruffled up and bothered.

Suddenly this face looked at me. Its eyes were bright green, shining in the moonlight, and it had a dog's face with two ears sticking up on either side of its head; its teeth were bared and there were a lot of them. He was red-furred, sharp-snouted and very bushy-tailed. I'd never seen a dog quite like him.

I growled. He barked, a ghastly heaving noise, and yet . . . sad.

'Get out,' I said. 'Clear out and leave these birds alone.'

He growled. I could see whatever he was he wasn't going to do what I said. Still these birds were flapping, cackling and screeching. He wriggled in under the wire and got hold of one of them. Then he bit the wretched thing's head off!

'I *say*!' I said. 'How revolting! Who do you think you are to go round biting bird's heads off?'

He stared at me.

'I'm a dog,' he said.

'A dog? What sort of a dog? You just stop it, or I'll bite the hell out of you – and I *can*!'

He stood staring at me again. 'I'm a wild dog, and I'm hungry.' Then he started on the others, and it was a massacre.

'You're the biggest Pig Dog I've ever met,' I shouted, 'and I know a lot of dogs. Personally, I wouldn't admit to you being a dog at all, taking advantage of all these birds – not only scaring them to death, but *sending* them to death.'

He shut his mouth, saliva was dripping from it.

'And let me tell you something else, I'm not afraid of you, and you're covered in fleas anyway.'

'I gotta live, haven't I?' he said.

'I see no reason why you should,' I replied, 'and don't you come near this bird in its bed, or I'll really have a go at you.'

The birds stopped cackling for a few moments, and watched.

'I hate your kind of dog,' he said. 'Like hounds and terriers, they chase us for miles, and when we get in our holes they dig us out and cut off our tails.'

'Well?' I asked, not quite sure what to say next.

'Well,' he said, 'how would you like it?'

'In the first place, I haven't got a tail – not that anyone would want to cut it off. And anyway, if you go about biting heads off birds and things, you deserve it.'

'Shut up,' he said, and picked up another bird!

'You flea-bitten dunghill Pig Dog!' I shouted, and flew at him. I got him by the throat, but he was too cunning and threw me off into this netting. I went for him again, and he got me in my bad leg.

'That's my lame leg!' I screamed.

'Who cares!' he said, and made for another wretched bird.

There was only one thing for it. I started barking and squealing, and if poor old Harold thinks he'd really heard me bark, I really went to town in a big way. I screamed the place down.

He went for me again. He bit my tail and threw me over his shoulder. I landed on this bird with all these yellow babies. He snapped one of them up whole! I thought I was going to be sick or die, but I hung on to him with my teeth until I thought they would all come out.

Suddenly I saw a torch, and two big Humans. He tried to get away, but I hung on to his tail.

'What the hell!' I heard one of these Humans say.

'Don't shoot yet, Simon, I think he's cornered.'

'It's a terrier!' the other Human said.

'Or a rat.'

I was so angry I let go. This wild dog tried to make a get-away through this hole in the netting. There was a sudden bang – must have been a bomb. I fell over, and as I did I saw this wild dog lying on the ground.

'Dead,' I thought. 'That's what he is, dead.' My jaw ached and I was covered in blood. I lay there exhausted. These two Humans stood over me. I wondered if they'd put a bomb on me too. I closed my eyes.

'It's not even a Jack Russell,' one of them said.

'Pretty gutsy to hang on to that vixen, poor little blighter.'

'What is he and what is he doing here?'

'He's some kind of a stray, but he's saved the lives of half these birds.'

One of them picked me up. He was very gentle. Not like a vet or Ben, that scarecrow of a man.

'Poor little devil, he hasn't half had a mauling, look at his ear.'

They shone the torch on me. Not even a Jack Russell! I thought. And who the heck is he, anyway? One of them mended the hole in the netting and picked up the two dead birds; they were all calmer now, but still gasped in fright.

'I'll take this little unsightly creature into Venetia,' the gentle Man said. 'She'll know what to do with it!'

They both laughed. I was beyond caring. I ached everywhere. The gentle Man put me under his coat, and we went off down a long path with these azaleas on either side, like we have at home.

'Hope he isn't too far gone,' said the other Human.

'She'll fix him up. Wonder where he came from?'

'Well, we finally got that ruddy fox, thanks to him.'

I kept on thinking of this wild dog, lying dead in the moonlight, and how he said he was hungry, and if you're hungry you could bite *anyone*'s head off. Mean to say, if I'd seen a mouse . . . Oh well! I reckoned I was really beginning to learn about taking care of myself, like Wellington and these hares. S'pose everyone goes for something smaller than themselves.

We came across a giant lawn, and beyond it was a really gigantic house, bigger even than my home. We went through a gigantic door, through a gigantic hall, into the *most* gigantic room. A beautiful mother sort of person got up from a sofa. She had long black hair and a bright green velvet dress, like She wears sometimes.

'Simon! Jamie! What was it all about?'

'That ruddy fox again.'

'Oh, not the baby chicks too?'

'No, only two old boilers. Their lives were literally saved by this stray who fought the brute off like a tiger!'

He opened his coat and displayed me.

'Oh! Poor little thing,' she said. 'What is it? Not a rat, I hope.'

Another Human lady came away from this gigantic fire. 'It's some sort of terrier, I think,' and she stroked my bloody head. I licked her hand.

'Poor little thing,' said the Green Lady. 'Call Dean and tell him to bath him, and then we'll have a look at his wounds.'

Bath! Not again! I thought, but I was too tired to care. They put me by this fire and pulled something on the wall. A man dressed like a penguin appeared.

'Yes, Your Grace?'

'Dean, this little feller has just had a battle with a fox.'

'A fox, Your Grace?'

'Found him hanging on to his tail in the chicken run.'

'Most unusual, Your Grace.'

'Most. I could have understood a Jack Russell. But, well, what is it?'

The Penguin scrutinized me carefully.

'One of them type of terriers, I'd say, Your Grace.'

'Well, take him away will you, and give him a good bath, and then we can see what he is and where he's hurt.'

'As you say, Your Grace.'

Your Grace handed me to this Penguin and he took me into some kind of wash-house where he gave me a good ducking with a shower like He has at home. Two other Human ladies came in to watch. Both wore white pinafores like Fred the Squirrel.

'My word, what next?' one of them said. 'Looks like a wet rat.'

'Pore thing,' said the other pinafore. 'I'll get a towel and then we'll see.'

''E must be pretty fierce because 'is Grace said 'e was fighting this fox in the chicken run.'

'Well I never! Brave, that's what 'e is!'

'For Gawd's sake, keep 'im away from that there Dana in case 'e upsets 'er.'

What *is* that Dana, I thought. I may upset that Dana, but that Dana isn't going to upset me. No one is after that wild dog. They rubbed me dry and one of them brushed me. I could see in a mirror that I looked pretty good, except for my torn ear. The Penguin took me back to this gigantic room.

'Ah,' said Your Grace.

'Ah!' said the fireplace lady. 'It's a Yorky!'

I could have kissed her – and did.

'Lady or gentleman?' she asked.

'Clearly a gentleman in every way, but where does he come from? What shall we do with him?'

'Someone must have lost him. Better tell the police in the morning.'

Police! I thought miserably, as I sat by the fire. That means being moved on. I growled slightly. They all laughed.

'Clearly he isn't keen on the police!'

'Any identification papers?'

'Nothing. Don't even know his name.'

'I shall call him Stray, as long as he's here,' said the Green Lady. 'And now we must get him something to eat, mustn't we Dean?'

The Penguin seemed to sigh slightly.

'Meat, biscuits, fresh asparagus?' he laughed.

They all laughed.

'Give him some of Jenny's Chum,' said the Green Lady. My heart fell, but I was so hungry I would have even eaten a chicken.

I ate it all up. Never again, I thought, if I ever get home, will I be mingy about that old tinned stuff She used to give me! Oddly enough, I wished it had been hedgehog soup with old Barmy and Wellington, and I couldn't help wondering how they were, and kind of missing them.

They put me in a basket and, as I was falling asleep in front of this warm gigantic fire, I heard one of them say, 'I wonder what Jenny will think of him?'

Your Grace laughed. 'Well, I suppose they'll both speak the same language, eh Simon?'

They were all still laughing when I fell asleep.

'D'you think he's house-trained?' I heard one of them say before I went out altogether.

When I woke up, it was quite light and I was alone. I was still in this gigantic room, and I had a good look round. There were flowers everywhere, and the walls were full of pictures of weird Humans with lace collars round their necks and men with long hair and peculiar clothes. I wandered about a bit to get rid of my stiffness. I was longing to take a leak, but it was clear that this was not the place to do it.

One of the apron ladies came in and pulled back the curtains. I looked out of the window. Wow! I thought. Fancy having a huge sheet of glass on this lawn.

'Want to go out, do you dearie?' she asked.

I wagged what was left of my tail.

She opened the window. 'There's a good little boy,' she said.

I went out over this large pavement and made for the sheet of glass, after I'd had a good leak of course. I'd learnt enough to have a good smell at this glass before I got too near. It was water! and there were birds floating about on it. Live birds! Two were really something – dead white, big, with great long necks. They came up to me and hissed something quite unintelligible. I backed off; I didn't like the look in their eyes.

Suddenly I heard a squeaky voice behind me. 'Who d'you think you are?'

I turned round and came face to face with a Toy Yorkshire! At first I was dumbfounded. Then I pulled myself together.

'I'm a visitor,' I said.

'Oh? Who invited you?'

'Your Grace did,' I replied haughtily. 'I'm the hero what saved the birds from the wild dog last night.'

'Tell me another.'

'I'm not going to waste my time with you if you don't believe me,' I replied. 'I am not in the habit of lying, nor do I have time for it.'

'La di da.'

'Who are you anyway?'

'I'm Lady Jennifer of Castle Cape.'

'Oh.'

'And who, may I ask, are you?'

'I'm not allowed to say,' I replied.

'I know who you are – you're Stray. I heard talk about you getting my Chum.'

'I didn't ask for your Chum. Matter of fact, I don't really care for your Chum or anyone else's Chum, but after my ordeal with the wild dog I was exceedingly hungry.'

'I see.'

I looked at this Lady Jennifer of Castle Coop or whatever it was. She was very pretty, I have to admit that. She was the smallest grown-up Toy I'd ever seen. Mean to say, she didn't look as if she'd ever grown! Her long silky hair was tied up on the top of her head with a pink ribbon and she had large brown eyes.

'You're a Yorkshire,' I said.

'Brilliant,' she replied.

'I'm one too,' I said.

'Clearly not a Pedigree,' she tossed her head.

'For your information, I have a very long pedigree, and my great grandfather was a champion, so there!'

'My mother and father were both champions,' she replied, taking a sip of water. 'Anyway, why do you look so awful? Look at your hair! And your ears don't stick up like mine.'

'In the first place, my hair hasn't been brushed for weeks and weeks. Secondly, my ears are not supposed to stand up, that's only for Toys. And lastly, one of them was nearly taken off during my fight saving *your* chickens.'

'Why hasn't your hair been brushed for weeks? What sort of people do you live with anyway?'

'I live with the most wonderful people in this world, but ...'

'Well?'

'I was lost ...'

Her eyes widened.

'... and I've been living with Gypsies, and I escaped and hid in your chicken run.'

'You kid me not!' she exploded.

'They put a heavy chain on me and tied me under their house on wheels.'

'My dear!' she said. 'Tell me more!'

'Then this boy took my collar away, so now I have no identification papers.'

'My dear!'

'I don't know what's going to happen to me. If I had to stay anywhere, I'd like to stay here, but Your Grace is going to tell those Police.'

'Then they'll find your people. They always do.'

'But I might be shut up in some old cell like a criminal for weeks while they try to find them.'

'True, too true ... I don't see how I can help you. I don't speak their language, though I understand it.'

'Me too.'

'Poor old Stray.'

'Anyway, my name isn't Stray. It's Chips.'

'Quite a common little name really.'

I was just about fed up with this little snob, I really was. I turned away.

'Look who's coming,' she sniggered.

About the biggest dog you've ever seen in your life emerged from the window. Huge, but HUGE!

'Whatever is that?' I asked.

'That is Dana, the mastiff,' she giggled.

'What are all those bubbles hanging down from her stomach?' I asked.

'Tits, dear, just tits.'

'Tits?'

'What she feeds the babies with.'

'What babies?'

'Hers, of course, you ass.'

'Where are they?'

'In her stomach.'

'How can she feed her babies with these tits if they're in her stomach?'

She rolled on the grass with laughter.

'They haven't come out yet, stupid!'

'When will they come out?'

'When they're good and ready to,' she replied. 'Only she knows, but she's getting ready in case it happens suddenly. She's very nice really. Slightly inane, but at least she can get her face up on the kitchen table and have a sniff at any grub going.'

I gave up.

I really had a ball in that place. To start with there was miles and miles of it. We used to follow Your Grace everywhere, the three of us, that is, though Dana was always behind. There were ponies and horses, cows and even sheep – what silly faces they have, poor things, and they run about all jammed together.

Your Grace used to take his gun and shoot at things. I liked him, I really did, and the Green Lady became the Pink Lady, the Lady in what's called a kilt and, at night, a most beautiful purple velvet dress. Sometimes her hair hung down, sometimes it was tied up and stuck on the back of her head. The food was really good. We had three bowls. I noticed Dana always had more than anyone else but, as Jenny told me, she was really feeding nine people! What a ghastly thought!

There were always hundreds of people there, laughing and eating, and once Jenny told me there was what they call a Royal, though honestly he didn't seem any different from anyone else, to look at I mean, though you could have called him very good-looking. I sat on his lap once, and he was very gentle and sweet to me, saying things like 'Poor Stray, where do you come from?' They all laughed at this and asked him his favourite type of dog. Unfortunately I was not among them; they were labradors, shootin' dogs and these corgis, which I have to say I'm not keen on. They nip you in the behind when you're not looking.

There were times I really loved – with just Jenny, knee-high to a bee, and Dana. We used to romp along the paths bordered by azaleas and rhododendrons, leak when we wanted to and smell around in the ground. I suppose we were a funny threesome to look at: first this huge Dana – weighing they told me 170 pounds – then myself and Jenny, in that order. Jenny looked like a mosquito compared with Dana, and yet her brain in some ways was sharper. Dana used to sit down a lot owing to her condition, and I have to say I found her conversation very interesting.

'What a huge room,' I said once.

'Very,' she replied.

'All them lace collars.'

'All *those* lace collars,' she said.

'Sorry.'

'Portrait by Justus Sistermans of Corsino Florence, 17th-century Bobbin lace, and then the gentlemen – 16th century . . .'

'Oh.'

'Very valuable, very old. Been in the family a great number of years.'

'Oh.' I thought I'd change the subject.

'You're a big dog, aren't you?'

'A very big dog, one of the biggest. I'm over thirty inches in height, and when my babies arrive, which is any minute, they'll be bigger than you when they're born.'

'Golly.'

'I like you, you know.'

'Thanks.'

'You're a terrier.'

'You bet your sweet life.'

'At the same time you're only a comparatively new terrier.'

'Eh?'

'Put it this way; oddly enough, you are linked with the mastiff group.'

'Oh good.'

'But now I'm talking about people like bull terriers, whippets, dalmatians, pointers ...'

'I know a whippet.'

She didn't appear to be listening.

'... airdales, Boston terriers, Welsh or Irish terriers, Scottish setters, then the short-legged terriers, Scottish, Cairns, West Highlands, English Fox terriers, Manchester terriers, Toy terriers, like Jenny and you.'

'Look here,' I said.

'You'd be one of those.'

'I am *not* a Toy terrier,' I said indignantly.

'There's nothing against them,' she said kindly. 'But, personally, I don't consider them much of a dog.'

'You great lump of wrinkled flesh,' I shouted. 'I'm as much of a dog as you are. I've got four legs haven't I?'

'So has a pig, or a sheep,' she said laconically.

I sat there looking and feeling very small. Words failed me.

'Poodles,' I suggested lamely.

'Idiots,' she replied. 'All tarted up like that Jenny.'

'Well?'

She heaved her huge bulk into a sitting position.

'You see, dear, you're a very new kind of a breed. 1800 at the best, a mixture of Skye and Manchester.'

'Very popular,' I hazarded.

'Very – they eat less. But you see, the real dog is more like the wild species, the wolf and the jackal, the fox ... they came from the Bronze Age. The Wolf, like the Alsatian. Now, my breed, the Mastiff, comes from the Babylonians which has altered in no way since BC to the present time.'

'BC?'

'Two thousand odd years ago. In those days, we were used for hunting. Now we're watch-dogs.'

'I'm considered a watch-dog.'

'We were used for bear-baiting and bull-baiting.'

'My grandfather was a champion, and my ancestor, Huddersfield Ben, was put to fighting monkeys and rats and baiting bulls!'

'Really?'

'D'you know what I think you are?'

'No...'

'I think you're a powerfully-built wrinkled old skin snob, and I'll tell you something else, I personally defeated one of your wretched wild species-in the chicken run.'

'Really?'

'Really. He was a jackal or a wolf or a fox, and...'

'Yes?'

'... a real pig dog, so don't sit there with all your tits showing and give me a lesson, because you bore the heck out of me.'

I walked away into the rhododendron bushes and sat down. I felt sick and angry. I was as good as she was. I could move faster. The plaster on my ear irritated me. I tapped my lame

foot on the ground. Oh! If I could only go home! Everyone was
so kind and sweet there – so ordinary, no penguins, no Your
Graces. I didn't even like the smell of the Green-Pink Lady.
What a battle life is, I thought to myself. Anyway, I didn't feel
all that good.

I decided to run away again. Heaven knows where. Then, to
my unutterable horror, I saw this Pink Lady walking towards
me with a policeman!

'Stray? Come on, Stray!' she wheedled.

I could only blow out my cheeks and sit there.

'You see, Sergeant, as I told you, we found him in the hen
house. He'd had a bit of a going over by this fox.'

'Stood up to a fox, did he?'

'Amazingly, yes! We've had him here for a few days and he's
recovered his wounds, poor little thing, but he must belong to
someone who's mourning his loss, so I thought I'd report him.'

'Quite right, Your Grace.'

Everyone round here seems to have the same name, I
thought.

'Perhaps you'd like to take him to the station while you find
his proper owners.'

'To tell you the truth, Your Grace, we're pretty well jammed
with dog life at the moment.'

'How sad.'

'Yes, well, you see, they get fed up with the feeding of them
and they *try* to lose them.'

'No!'

'Indeed, yes. Why, we had one case where it was reported to
us that a man opened his car door, popped this labrador out
and went on driving.'

'How disgusting!'

'It's the inflation.'

'They shouldn't have the dog in the first place.'

'Right.'

'Well, what do you suggest?'

'My advice to you is to keep the little blighter here. We'll
make enquiries around, and let you know.'

'All right, Sergeant. We've plenty of room and food for him here, haven't we, Stray?' She picked me up and I licked her face.

'I think that would be in order, Your Grace,' he said. 'The poor little blighter would only end up in a compound of barking dogs!' He laughed grimly as if the whole thing was a terrible burden to him.

'And', she said, 'if you don't find the owner, we might find a friend who would like to take him over.'

'Well,' he said, 'I hope we do but, as I say, so many people today don't want to claim them any more.'

'Thank you, Sergeant,' she said, and he turned on his heel and left.

'Poor little Stray,' she said. 'Has someone thrown you away?'

'No! No!' I barked. 'They loved me. I just don't know where I am, and I have no identification papers!'

'Ssh,' she said. 'We mustn't wake up Granny, must we?' She hadn't understood a word I'd said.

I followed her round the glass water while she threw bread to the birds. They all do that, I thought. She did that, only She didn't have any glass water. There was a man there bending over the flower-bed. He could have been Harold, but he wasn't ... I stared down at myself in the glass water. I certainly had aged a great deal and, though I'd learnt a lot about life, it was mostly sad.

Days and nights passed. I got on very well with Jenny, who only seemed interested in how many fleas the fox had on him. Then, one day, an American lady came to stay. She was a very happy person, everything was 'just marvellous'. She took a liking to me for no good reason except that I was brushed and combed.

'Jean dear,' she said one night, 'if nobody claims that stray, I'd just lerve to take him home to Boston.'

'Why not?' said Your Grace. 'He's been here quite a long time and no one has claimed him, and frankly ... well, Jenny is going to be in a certain condition pretty soon ...'

'Why then, it's a deal,' she said.

I asked Jenny about this statement.

'Oh, you know,' she said. 'They're just worried you might fall in love with me.'

'So what if I do?'

'Well, it's up to me, isn't it my dear?'

'In what way?'

'I have to stick to the Aristocracy. Mean to say, I have to fall in love with another Toy.'

'Do you know one?'

'Actually I do, but he's awful. A sort of social playboy. He's called Rudolph of Henteau – rather a cad.'

'Well?'

'Well, my dear Chips, as you'll learn, where there's one there is always another. I have my eye on another.'

'I see.'

'No doubt at all that one day my Prince will come down the gravel path, or through the front door.'

'I see.'

'My dear, we really only fall in love with our own kind. When we don't, it all goes wrong.'

'I see.'

'Anyway, you aren't in love with me and...'

'I think you're the prettiest dog I ever saw, but at the moment my mind is in such a poor state that I can't really settle down to any romanticism.' (I kept quiet about Tina and all those kids!)

'Anyway, darling, we wouldn't be allowed to, we aren't *quite* the same breed – see what I mean?'

I went off by myself for a two-mile walk. I was beginning to feel so dreary that I wondered if I was in for a nervous breakdown.

Suddenly, one day, something happened! They were getting this big lunch going in the kitchen. We were shoved out into the garden in case we got 'under their feet'. Cars arrived with people all dressed up in them.

'It's Your Grace's birthday,' Jenny told me.

They were all laughing and cracking jokes, carrying glasses of fizzy water, and snapping their fingers at us, especially Jenny who looked absolutely beautiful. We'd both had the inevitable bath, but somehow I didn't come out looking so good, though one of the ladies said what lovely sad eyes I had. Better than nothing, I thought...

'Hullo there!' called Your Grace from the garden, and started walking towards the gigantic room. Two people came out. I could not believe it – it was Him and Her!

I was positively rooted to the ground. I was certain I was dreaming. I could see my reflection in the glass water, and I looked rough in spite of my bath. I stared at them. I *knew* it was them, because for one thing I knew that dress spotted with blue flowers. They were both laughing with Your Grace, talking and drinking this fizzy stuff.

I couldn't move. Don't ask me why. Then I began to shiver.

'Got a cold?' Jenny asked. 'Because if you have, keep away from me.' And she trotted towards them.

'Come on, Jenny,' said Your Grace.

They smiled and turned towards her. Their smiles changed, and together they walked slowly towards me.

'It can't be,' They said together.

'How could it?' He asked.

I sat shivering by the glass water, looking up at Them.

'It *could* be,' She said. She knelt down on the grass beside me. 'Chippo?' she queried. 'Chippo?'

I flung myself at them. I scrambled all over them, kissing, dancing in circles, standing on my head, barking and barking, holding their fingers in my mouth, like I always used to. She held me in her arms, kissing and stroking me.

The Pink Lady came across the grass smiling.

'I see Stray has taken to you, darling!' she laughed.

'Stray?' He questioned.

'Well, we call him Stray. He came to us out of the blue in the middle of the night – quite extraordinary really. He was in the chicken run and had had a fight with this fox and...'

'Fox!' He said.

'But...' She stuttered. 'He's our Mr Chips! We'd recognize him anywhere.'

I barked madly, and stared at them with all the love I could muster.

'How amazing!' said the Pink Lady. 'And how absolutely wonderful!'

'He must have lost himself when we were on location. We've been searching for him for ages.' She hugged me. He hugged me.

'He looks so well!'

'We've taken great care of him, and been waiting for the police to report a lost dog.'

Lost dog, I thought, that's what I've been, but I jolly well won't be lost again! Everyone seemed very happy about it all and raised their glasses to 'Mr Chips!'.

I kept very close to Them while they all walked round the glass water, and sat under Their feet while they were eating and people were talking about their experiences of 'lost dogs'.

At the end of the party we got into this gleaming dark blue car belonging to Your Grace. There was a golden angel flying ahead of us on the front. I felt safe and happy. I was going home. They were all there to see us off, grinning and waving.

'Goodbye, Jenny,' I shouted.

'It's a world of Hullo and Goodbye,' she grinned.

7 Dognapped

I WAS GIVEN another bath, of course, and brushed. I was also given a few Good Boy Chocolates, which I don't really like, some vitamin pills and, believe it or not, a bone! I sat in my big basket and surveyed the kitchen while She was cooking something called curry.

I always consider this kitchen to be the heart of the house. It's always warm and full of people drinking coffee. I love the smells and the hope I'll get some pieces of beef when She makes this casserole. Sometimes He has a go, especially at spaghetti, which He thinks is His great number. The last time He made it, it was like rope, and even the Koo Koos got their beaks stuck. Now He cooks egg and bacon and mushrooms, which smells good, but I don't get much of it as they wolf the whole lot Themselves. He says He can't bear waste, so He stuffs Himself with much more salad than He needs. What They see in salad I do not know, it's just slimy green stuff to me.

It's no ordinary kitchen this: it's decorated with pictures and amusing pots, a knife from a Bedouin Chief and a fan some Arab gave Her in the Desert. Some of the pictures are funny because they were painted by the Beautiful Daughters and the Grand Sons, like one which shows mice chasing the cook. There's a Fly Swat from Thailand that I'd like to get hold of too.

Sometimes that old Robin comes in and sits on the table and eats the sugar. Harold comes in dead on eleven o'clock, and again at four, for his tea and coffee. There's no need to look at the clock, he's always there at the right time. At other times there are about eight people drinking coffee, like Electricians, Carpet-cleaners and Eric, who's made this new goldfish pool, and they all go away with their cars stuffed with apples.

I went out with Them into the garden, to the bird table. There seemed to be hundreds of Sparrers, and I flew at them because it's the Koo Koos table. She stopped me.

'Not a sparrer will fall but "he" will know it,' She said reprovingly. Who 'he' is I don't know, but honestly there are millions of them, so why should 'he' even care?

While I've been away, this old Pussy Willow has been cut down, and that's where the fish pond is. It's not finished yet – mean to say, there aren't any fish to catch, but He said: 'Suddenly the garden will be full of Herons eating the goldfish. They even go and find them in Gerrards Cross.'

'The death of that tree has changed the birds' routine,' She said. 'For instance, the Koo Koos go to the Big Yew now. They don't sit much on the Tree of Life.'

'That's only because there aren't many leaves left and the Yew is warmer,' He told Her.

I was quite astonished to see about sixty Koo Koos, and I chased them. She explained that the big house in the park had spotlights on all night, so they had to roost in the Yew tree. Then they would come and eat all our apples. She called them 'the angels'.

'Phew,' I thought. 'The weight will bring that old tree down.' But it hasn't so far.

They took me everywhere with them after I came back – Gerrards Cross, of course, but I was left in the car (locked in as a matter of fact) while They did Their shopping. When Ace, number two Grand Son, came to the house he had to put me on a lead because he has the habit of nipping out through this lych-gate as he is as keen on the graveyard as I am.

Well, as I said, I went everywhere with Them even to

people's houses, and restaurants. I have to say I behaved well. I didn't chase cats or leak on the furniture.

Then we went to dreaded London. I was forced into a bag She carried round Her shoulders. I felt a twerp but I did what She told me to, and the smells round the lamp-posts were most interesting. I know why, because I saw what they call an Arab relieving himself on one of them. He had on this long white nightgown, in broad daylight! One big dog did it on my head, and got a good whack with Her umbrella.

This never-to-be-forgotten day, we went to this Big Store. I was in Her bag as usual, having a good look round as She paused at this and that before She met Him for lunch. The nice man who sat among coats and hats and umbrellas usually shared his food with me – what there was, which was mostly cheese. I was looking forward to that.

She had to go to the loo, so She told me. She can't do it on a lamp-post, She told me, it wouldn't be right. It doesn't seem so important to Him, though I've never seen Him do anything on a lamp-post. I have seen Him do it on these Begonias in the dark and he really got a wigging. So, She went to this place called 'Ladies'. She put me on the floor and I got out of the bag for a stretch and mosey about. She was too engrossed in what She was doing to notice that a hand came under this Loo, pulled my lead and suddenly I was through on the other side! A strange Human girl picked me up in her arms and ran for her life. I could hear Her screaming, but by this time this Human girl and I were down the stairs and she was running like mad along the street and into a taxi. The next thing I knew was that we were in some room and I was standing there astonished, and she was lying on this bed in her red skirt, roaring with laughter!

'We done it, Baby,' she said. 'Like a drinka water?'

She gave me some water in a saucer and I drank it.

'Good baby,' she said. She lay on the bed, lit a cigarette and went on laughing.

Another girl came into the room. She had green hair and no pants on.

'Look, Lettice, I got meself a dawg!' And she went off into gales of laughter again.

'Oh Mavis, you are a one and no mistake,' said Green Hair. 'How you done it?'

'Easy. Saw this lead sticking out from under the john, so I pulled it and he come out cool as brass, so I legged it down the stairs and hopped in here, easy done.'

'He's a nice little thing and all. Could do you credit.' Then they both laughed.

'And when I'm sleeping you can have him,' said the giggling one.

'He's a nice baby boy, isn't you a nice baby boy?'

I sat down on this carpet. It was very threadbare; it was yellow, green and purple, and made my eyes ache a bit, but it was different and it was very cold. I wagged my tail and licked the Green Hair.

'Look! He's friendly! Ooh, and look at his lovely collar and lead!'

They reminded me of the Gypsies, and I felt happier. No more bag-carrying, just a slow walk along strange alleyways with one or the other in their odd skirts up above their knees – not like Her or Your Grace. We went to lovely pubs and all drank beer. I love beer now. They had a lot of friends and everyone was always laughing and cuddling me. There was another dog in this Crown and Anchor pub. I watched him leak on all the table legs, but no one seemed to care. He never spoke to me.

'Come on, lovey, up on my lap, lovey,' she said.

I jumped up and did what she said.

'Well trained, innit?'

The man with her looked at me dubiously.

'He's a pedigree Yorky, shouldn't wonder.'

''Course he is, aren't yer, lovey?'

I licked her face. Safest thing to do. I was totally at sea and had no idea where I was or where They were.

'Wanta watch the fuzz, duckie?' this man said, and gave me some more beer. My head was a bit woozie. I didn't care any

more about anything. I just knew I was going to go on being lost
for the rest of my life, so I'd better make the best of it and hope I
didn't fall over like the man in the corner.

'Come on, lovey,' she said. 'Let's go, shall we? Shall we go
and see what we can catch?'

I had no idea what she meant, but I went with her immedi-
ately.

'Take care,' the man shouted, and they all laughed some
more.

We went off down this dark lane. She very kindly waited for
me to have a leak or two. Then this van drew up.

'Wanta lift, darling?' a man inside the van said.

'You betcher,' she said, and climbed in, dragging me with
her.

'Tell me about yourself, darling,' he said.

'Nothing much to tell. I'm in the Official Secrets,' she said.

He laughed. 'What do you say to a nice bit of chow and a jar
or two?' he asked.

'Okay by me, but no funny business or my dog will get you,' she said.

'What, that little cur?' he answered, and laughed again. Come to think of it, he laughed a great deal.

'He's a pedigree Yorkie,' she said.

'Must have cost you a bomb.'

'He did.'

'Where d'you get that kind of bomb?' he asked.

'Wouldn't you like to know,' she laughed.

'He don't need that expensive harness.'

I sat in the back and looked round. It was a sort of van I'd never seen. I kept falling over; I supposed it was the beer. We seemed to go a long way for this 'jar' as he called it. I wondered why, as I knew most of these pubs by now – the Crown and Anchor, the Swan, the White Horse, the Cow. What was he up to, this laughing man? They were talking all the time; their voices grew louder.

'Look here,' he said, 'what's bothering you?'

'Nothing really ... nothing I can think of offhand.'

We stopped at one of those motorway joints and they had something to eat. He took this flask out of his pocket and passed it to her.

'Always carry some cold comfort,' he said, and laughed again. Then they got back into this van.

'Where d'yer live?' he asked.

'Any old where,' she giggled.

'Okay,' he said in a loud voice. 'My place.'

'Suit yerself,' she said.

I have to say I was a bit browned off. I hadn't had anything to eat for hours. I thought of Him and Her and all the good food I used to get, and Your Grace, and Home, and even the hedgehog soup. Your place, I thought, that means I shall sit here for hours, and it's cold ...

Curiously, we stopped by a wood. A very dark wood.

'I'm not gettin' out here,' she said.

'Oh yes you are, my girl,' he said.

'Listen, I'm not that sort.'

'What sort? You're all the same sort: eat, drink and be merry and then pay nothing.'

They struggled together for quite a long time. She called 'Help' loudly a couple of times, but there was nobody there but me. I went for him, I really did. I bit his coat and snarled at him, but he was more fierce than the wild dog and threw me across this van and took my collar off me. Then he bundled this screaming girl out and marched her into this wood. What was I to do? I was shut in this van, getting colder and hungrier every moment. I sat there. No one passed by; no one. I remember the sky was a sort of night blue. I looked up into the hanging trees and thought of home. There were lights around, but they were in the distance. It was very lonely and really freezing. In her haste she'd left her jacket behind, so I snuggled into it and got warmer.

It got darker, and darker, and darker.

A car drove up to me. It had a blue light on top of it. I knew, oh I knew – it was a police car, I sat still in her jacket.

'What's this?' one of them said.

'Your guess is as good as mine.'

'Well, then, better get on with it.'

I barked. I tried to tell them about the man and this girl, but of course they didn't understand a word.

'Pretty silly leaving a jacket with a dog in it,' said one.

'Just tread careful, Albert,' said the other. 'Got your torch?'

'Lock the car up.'

'Okay.'

'Ruddy thick.'

'Yes, and a fog coming up.'

They disappeared. I sat there in her jacket. Pretty soon this van guy came back. He tried to get into the car but it was locked. He swore something terrible. Then he took a great stone and smashed the window, crawled across the front, got a really nasty grip on me – although I tried to hold on to the jacket for warmth – and, believe it or not, flung me into the road and made off, jacket and all. There was nothing for it but to sit beside this police move-on car. I did just that. I sat there for a long time. I was shivering. Pneumonia, I thought. I leaned against the wheel.

They came back at last, these two policemen.

'Got away,' said one.

'Must have smashed the front glass. We had the key.'

'Left this lot behind.'

'What lot?'

'The dog.'

'He could tell us a tale or two if he could only speak.'

I barked. I tried to tell them, but they didn't speak my language.

'Should have had the sniffer dog,' they said.

'Hey, listen, get on to 385 and tell them to send the sniffer dogs.'

'What's the use?'

'These dogs have their own common language.'

'You kill me!'

'Do it.'

'Okay, why not?' He picked up something and mumbled into it. We waited.

'Put the poor little chap into the car; he's freezing.' They put me into the car.

Suddenly three of these cars arrived with their blue lights blazing and their sirens shrieking. About ten men got into a huddle and talked. Then they let out these Alsations! Was I glad I was in a car. Someone took me out and put me on the ground. I stared at this Alsatian, and he stared at me.

'Go on,' he said.

'Go on what?' I asked.

'Where did they go?'

'Down there.'

'Grass or lane?'

'Lane, I think.'

'Make up your mind.'

'Grass,' I said, 'and call me Sir.' Really, they were dog policemen!

'He's our only witness, and hopeless and witless,' the police said.

What could I say or do? These Human idiots understand nothing but their own language. Mean to say, we understand every word *they* say, why in heaven's name can't we have a universal language? Mean to say, we could all understand each other then and help each other.

I leaned against the wheel of this car. What to do, I thought. Shall I scaper? But where to? On the other hand, if I hung about I might get something to eat, even if it meant a police cell.

I stayed there. I was stiff with cold and soaked. It was raining hard. I could see all this big water coming down from the lank trees in the car lights. I knew I must be looking like a wet rat by this time. An old pigeon squawked past me. I waited patiently. The rubber wheel was quite comforting and I knew someone would come back. The rain dripped into my eyes. I wished I was back in the bag or at home, but I was beginning to think I'd never see that house again. I had to face the fact that I was a destitute wanderer: without resources, in need of food and shelter, devoid of everything, going from place to place aimlessly, without settled route or destination – never mind love or affection. I wasn't even an adventurer like Jonathan.

I just sat there. I wished I was dead. My bad leg was aching, and my bad ear was sore, though in a funny way the rain seemed to be doing it good. I thought, I'm the loneliest, saddest, smallest animal in the entire world. Nothing to eat, nothing warm to sleep on – just mud and rain, and long lanky trees who couldn't care less.

They all came back at last. All these policemen and these Alsatians. I wagged my tail furiously. No one noticed. The Alsatian sniffer dogs were very pleased with themselves and kept bashing each other over the ears. I might as well not have been there as far as anyone was concerned. They carried a red skirt and some odd bits of clothing.

'Well, now it's for the forensic chaps,' they said, whatever that meant. 'It's an open and shut case as far as we're concerned – same old story.'

I seemed to have seen that red skirt before and said so. This policeman looked down at me.

'Why can't you give us a good description, chum?' he asked.

I did. I went into the whole thing.

'They don't half yap, this breed,' he said to his mate.

The Alsatians understood. They barked out my story to these two fools.

'That's enough, Silver, Sam. Quiet. Heel.' These dogs rolled their eyes to heaven and got into the car behind this wire cage.

'What shall we do with Yapper?' one of the policemen asked.

'Can't leave him here, can we? Cruel that is. Take him back with us of course – your kids might like to play with him for a bit.'

Play with me!

'What, with Silver and Sam?'

'Okay, if they don't eat him!' They all got into their cars. I sat on one of the policemen's lap. He stroked my sopping coat.

'Poor little thing, he does look bad,' he said, and they started talking among themselves. I looked back at these two Alsatians – terrifying really, with huge panting mouths covered in spit, their tongues lolling out at the side of their mouths. 'Okay, if they don't eat him,' he'd said. Horrors! They could eat me in one fell swoop, and no one would know where I'd gone! I started thinking of yet another escape. These children! I'd create a diversion like Barking and Wellington had done. What sort of house would it be? Grand, like Your Grace's, or small with this patio I'd never seen, or heavenly like home?

We stopped at the Police Station. I was taken in and they looked me over.

'No joy here,' said another policeman with a lot of stripes all over his hat. 'Hasn't even got any identification. What is he? Looks like an amiable rat to me.'

Rat! I could have gone for his trousers, but decided to play it cool. He clearly was *not* a vet.

'Anyway, Albert, take him back to Joyce and the kids for a while. He and Sam and Silver can have a good meal.'

'Like Yorkshire Hot Pot,' said another and they all laughed.

We went to a nice white house with flowers all round it, and some cement pavings. This, I thought, is the patio. The two Alsatians were put in a sort of kennel with wires round it, but I was taken into the house, which was small and very clean and homely. A lady came over to me; she was very pretty and had an apron on.

'Oh Albert, whatever have you got there?' she asked.

'Poor little thing was left on the site. Needs a good meal.'

'*And* a good bath,' she sniffed.

I stood my ground, trying to be as dignified as any Yorkshireman would have done. I wagged my tail, I licked her hand, I looked as pathetic as I knew how, and boy, was I beginning to know how . . . I had to hold on to myself after all my adventures. Jamboree seemed a hundred years ago, and I was beginning to forget all the people I'd known.

·She plunged me into this sink and washed me with Fairy soap. Silly, I thought, she'll never get the soap out. I lay helpless in the sink and tried to smile..She took me into the vegetable plot so that I could shake myself, and then she dried me with a tea cloth!

'There now,' she said, 'you look quite different, you poor little mite.' Then she brushed me with a scrubbing-brush which tore the hairs of my stomach, but I said nothing because I was waiting for this food.

'What shall we call him?' she asked over her shoulder. This policeman, Albert, was drinking beer and reading the paper.

'Yapper,' he said, without looking up.

Yapper. Oh dear, the names I've had. If only I could have been an MI5 agent; if they could only have understood my language as I did theirs. Why, I might have been given the George Cross.

She gave me something out of a tin. It smelled bad, but I was so hungry I could have eaten ten dead mice. She found me a cat basket and put a rug in it. I was reeling, I really was. I fell asleep, but what terrible dreams! Him and Her searching, the girl, the man, the van, the broken window. If only I had had the guts to hold on to her jacket, and what happened anyway?

'Know something?' said Albert to the lady, next morning at breakfast.

'What?' I heard her say.

'Got an idea who it might be.'

'Who?'

'Johnson. Now, if I could get a line-up, I bet this Yapper would recognize him.'

'Is it enough?'

'It's a start.'

'He's not exactly an Alsatian.'

'They're pretty cute, these young dogs. Could have been on a lead when he picked her up. He'd know him, I betcher.'

I slept for a long time. I thought I had bronchitis. My leg hurt me and so did my ear. When the kids came back from school, they fell on me.

'Can't we keep him, Mum?' they asked.

'If no one claims him. He's a dear little thing.'

There were two of them: a girl called Rosie and a boy called Dick. They were very gentle, though Dick pulled me behind his bicycle and I hated that. I was too weak, I was really.

'Let the poor little chap recover,' she said, 'and then I'll take him to the vet.' Vet! Oh, not again!

I lay in the sun on this patio and looked up at the trees – chestnuts, lilac, laburnum and tall roses. They reminded me of home. It's a huge place, with Him cutting the orchard, and Her weeding and watering the flowers; a place where life seemed so peaceful, and there were only the Koo Koos and Fred to worry about. Where were they all now, and did they think of me and wonder if I were dead?

In the evening Silver and Sam were allowed to come into the kitchen. The kids loved them and rode on their backs, they were so very friendly. I couldn't believe they were the same dogs. I grinned at them. They glared at me.

'Now Silver, Sam,' she said. 'This is poor Yapper who was in

on the whole incident. Be kind to him. He's very small and I
don't think he's well.'

They looked me up and down. 'We sniff out these dirty jobs,'
said Silver in my ear, 'but people like you are useless.'

'Leave him alone,' said Sam.

They scared me. They were so beautiful, so very frightening,
and when they wagged their tails, they knocked the plates off
the table.

'I wish I was an Alsatian,' I said to Sam. 'You remind me of
the fox I fought at Your Grace's.'

'We're wild dogs,' said Sam.

'I think you're ... smashing.'

He stared at me as he was munching his huge bone, as big as
me. He had an enormous mouth, a huge body and waving tail,
and yet this small child was pulling his long ears.

'We're the Police, you know.'

'Yes, sir.'

'We're trained for months. We have an Owner and we love him.'

'Yes, sir. So do I love mine.'

'Don't be a silly billy. We know your sort: indulged, undisciplined, rolling in some lady's rose garden. We're on the job morning, noon and night, to catch murderers, thieves and rapists.'

'I see.'

'Of course you don't. You don't even know what we're talking about, silly twit. We *scare* people!'

'Yes, sir.'

'You don't.'

'No, sir.'

'They can kick you if you bark, but if we bark, they run like hell.'

'Yes, sir.'

'Take this case . . . this woman has been murdered, worse . . .'

'Oh no!'

'Why oh no?'

'I didn't know. I was shut in this van. I just waited.'

'Just another maniac. Let me tell you, Yapper, there's no maniacs in the animal world. Animals just kill to eat, not to damage.'

'Right, sir.'

'We sniff that type out, the *stupid* killers. We're taught to sniff out drugs too, in the Police Force.'

'I wish I could be in the Police Force,' I said.

They rolled about laughing. Then Sam said, thoughtfully, 'You know, we're the big chaps, but these small chaps could be very useful underground.'

'Really?' sniffed Silver.

'They could memorize things – faces, places, car numbers . . .'

'I can always remember faces and places,' I said, 'but car numbers! Mean to say, I've got no reason to remember car numbers. Except one, I do remember one. I hit my bad ear on it after the fox . . .'

'Don't go into a great saga. What colour was the car? And what was the number?'

'What does it matter? Don't know what car it was, but it was a short number.'

'In our job anything can lead to something.'

'Well, I think I'm right when I say...'

'No use thinking you're right in a court of law.'

I took a stab at it: 'E-B-I,' I said triumphantly.

'E-B-I,' mused Sam. 'What colour?'

'Blue, I'm sure it was blue.'

'What make?' asked Silver.

'I told you I don't know makes, but it had a long funnel in front.'

'S'pose you mean a bonnet!' Silver scoffed.

'Go easy, Silver, don't scare the littel mongrel,' said Sam. Mongrel! I closed my eyes.

'Any distinguising marks on the bonnet?'

'I remember, sir, there was a flying angel. I'll always remember.'

'Never mind your thoughts. Flying angel, Sam?'

'Roller of course. A blue Roller.'

'So what? As I said, I was taken into this Big Store and then the Red Skirt bagged me from under the wall of the Loo.'

'Red Skirt? That's what we found in the wood, Silver.'

'Our bloke might like that piece of evidence.'

'I think it was Your Grace's car, she was always in it ... anyway how can we tell them? They can't understand.'

'Good thinking.'

I started to shiver as an idea struck me.

'The poor little chap is cold,' said Sam.

'I'm not a little chap, and I'm not cold. The boy, how old is he?'

'Five.'

'I can tell him. He'll understand me.'

'Why?'

'He's not as high as the top of the sofa.'

Silver stretched himself out and laughed. 'Find him then!'

I found the boy playing with his bike, wagged my tail and walked up to him. The other two followed.

'Can you write?' I asked the boy.

'Some,' he said.

'Here's a crayon.'

'It's mine.'

'Can you write the letters I tell you?'

'Why?'

'It's important.'

'Why?'

'Sam and Silver want you to.'

'Why don't you do it?'

'Can't write.'

'What is it?'

'A car number – E-B-I.'

He wrote it on the flagstone with this pink crayon. Sam charged into the house and brought out Albert.

'What's your game, Dickie?' he asked.

'It's a car.'

'E-B-I – what car?'

'Yapper's car.'

'How can Yapper say that?'

'He just did.'

A few days later two constables and Albert came for me. It's jail this time, I thought, as they looked at me with curiosity. They put me into the car with the blue light and drove off.

We went for miles. I just sat and stared at the passing fields and villages. They seemed to be watching me, and I can tell you I was beginning to get anxious. We came to these gates and swept up a long drive that I remembered. When we reached the house, it seemed very dead to me: all the shutters were closed, the garden was dank – mind you, it was the beginning of winter and there were leaves everywhere.

Albert rang the doorbell several times, but no one came, not even the Penguin man. The policemen wandered about the garden with me on a lead. We came to a little house where a frightened-looking man opened the door.

'His Grace?' Albert enquired.

'They're away in Australia for three months,' the man said. 'The house is closed up. I'm the gardener.'

'Seen this Yorkshire terrier before?' Albert asked.

'Oh yes, sir, that'll be Stray. His owners come and take him away some weeks ago.'

'What were the owners' names?'

'Dunno, sir.'

Jenny appeared from nowhere. 'You smelly old tramp,' she laughed. 'Have you been arrested?'

'On the contrary,' I said. 'We're on a murder hunt.'

'You kill me with your stories!'

They put me back in the car. I felt sick.

'Well,' said Albert. 'We'll have to keep him for the line-up, and hope.'

8 An Older and Wiser Dog

I WAS SOON to know what a line-up was! Human degradation, I call it. These two Alsatians and I were taken some place, don't ask me where, and there, in front of us, was this line of Human Beings, standing there, just standing, about eight of them. Some were grinning scornfully, others staring at nothing. They were dilapidated, dirty, unshaven, like people about to be shot on this awful telly.

I was pulled along by Albert on a huge lead that clearly belonged to one of the Alsatians, who I'm here to tell you walked behind me for once. This Albert walked me up and down this line of horrors, and they all laughed! I didn't know what I was supposed to do. I looked back at Silver and yawned.

'You said you wished you were in the Police Force, Yapper.'

'So?'

'Well, *do* something!'

'What the heck am I supposed to do with this lot?'

'You are supposed to recognize someone, idiot.'

'The man who took the Red Skirt into the wood, of course!'

'Oh ...'

'Well, get on with it. We don't want to march up and down as if it was trooping the colour! When old Albert lets you off your string, you just go straight up to anyone you have seen before and bark. Understand, twit?'

'Yes, sir.'

Albert stood still, so did the other policemen, and Sam and

Silver sat down. I took a quick leak and sat down too. Then Albert walked slowly along the line saying the Humans' names out loud. I followed at a discreet distance.

'What's this rat got to do with us then,' said one of them. Well, quite apart from being pretty livid, I recognized his voice. It was the same voice I had heard in the van, though I have to be honest I couldn't really remember his face. Well, I flew at him for calling me a rat, and barked so hysterically that Albert had to pick me up.

'That's him,' he said. 'Johnson.' He sort of hissed the name.

These Humans were herded out, and we went in another direction.

'Pretty good that, eh?' asked the other policeman.

'Yapper is no slouch. He should be a useful member of the force,' answered Albert. 'Good boy,' he said and patted me on the head. Then he put me down among these Alsatians.

'Okay?' I asked Silver.

'You were lucky the chap called you a rat,' he answered.

'Not at all,' I replied loftily. 'I was pretty sure of him all the time.'

'No kidding!' said Sam, and they both laughed.

At the Police Station a man took a photograph of me, don't ask me why.

'What did he do that for?' I asked Silver as we went home.

'You'll be in the criminal record-book now,' he told me.

'No one took my fingerprints,' I answered.

'Your fingerprints must be *something*,' said Sam, 'like an ant's I shouldn't wonder!'

I was given the same food as they had, and nearly burst trying to eat it.

'Clever as a monkey, that Yapper,' I heard Albert say to Joyce.

I was more determined than ever to find Him and Her, even if it took me my lifetime. Him and Her and Me. We belonged together in that dear huge old rambling house with Fred and Harold and the Koo Koos.

I decided to tell the Alsatians.

'Understood,' they both said together.

'But what about my trail? You'll scent me out and I might get a whacking.'

'Not if you don't want us to. It's up to us what we scent out.'

'Oh ...'

'There's a blind lady lives about four doors away. She gets her Meals on Wheels, and she's really nice. You could hide up there while we go the other way,' said Silver.

'Thanks,' I said.

They turned their backs, and I went.

I counted two, three, four houses as I went. The door of the fourth house was open. It was a nice little white house and there were roses hanging all over the doors, which were open. I hesitated in case it was a trap – you see, I had begun to grow up. I did a couple of leaks on the box hedge, and then I wandered into the house. This rather dear old lady was lying in bed, staring at the ceiling. Her eyes were closed, and she was smiling. I wondered what she was smiling about.

'Who's that?' she asked.

I stared at her. I couldn't say anything she would have understood. There was only one thing to do, and that was to get on to her bed. I did just that. She put her hand out and touched my head. I licked her hand.

'Hullo, Doggie,' she said. 'You *are* a wet doggie, aren't you?'

I sat beside her on the bed without moving or scratching.

'You see, Doggie, I'm blind, so I can't see you. I can't even see what kind of Doggie you are. I know you're furry, I know you're a small doggie, a kind doggie ...'

She felt me all over and I sat quite still.

'You have longish hair, especially on your head, and no tail – I think you're a Yorkshire terrier!'

I licked her hand like mad.

'That's what you are! A dear little Yorky! But where did you come from? And why did you come to me? Are you hungry, dear? Well, if you wait a while the Meals on Wheels will come and we can share what they bring, can't we?'

I sat on the pillow beside her. I put out my bad arm and she stroked it. I looked at her. She was not so very old, but she had the most beautiful face, and she seemed to smile all the time. Her eyes were not closed, she just stared at the ceiling. They were green, her eyes were, but there was a large part in the middle that was white. She moved her hands about a lot and seemed pleased that she could stroke me. I think it was then that my idea of Human Beings changed. If I hadn't this great love for Him and Her, I would probably have stayed with this lady forever and learned to be her guide dog.

Pretty soon, these Meals on Wheels appeared. They knocked at the door and called, 'Valerie, it's us, dear.'

'Get under the clothes,' she told me, 'in case they take you away.'

I flew under her sheets, and nearly died of asphyxiation. A lot of talking and laughter went on, and then they left, closing the door. I ate as little as I could, though I was starving, because it didn't seem fair. They had left her some beer, and I had a sip of that too, but she didn't seem to want to take a leak or leave her bed. Later, there was a great sunset, which I was so sad she couldn't see.

But what to do? I wanted to go back to the Alsatians and tell them my dilemma. She talked to herself a great deal, about blackbirds and blackberries. She said she was as blind as any noon-tide owl, she said she was lonely and old, she talked of the country of the blind too, the waters of Lethe, and all sorts of things I didn't understand. I felt trapped. I had never been in such a ghastly position. I didn't know what to do or where to go.

I jumped off the bed.

'Doggie,' she said, 'don't leave me.'

I sat with my head against the door and my eyes closed. How unkind can you be to anyone? Mind you, she didn't know me or see me. I mean, I wasn't hers. Mean to say, I was only a passing stranger, listening to her confidences and eating her food – though not much of it. What to do? I decided to go back to the Alsatians, and did.

I sat in the garden and waited. No one seemed to be at home.
Pretty soon, however, they came back with Albert.

'Oh, it's you again,' they said in chorus.

'Yapper is back!' Albert cried. Joyce was pleased. She gave
me a good meal, but I was clearly unhappy. I just sat staring
into space.

'Pull your finger out,' Silver said.

'I can't,' I said. 'I think I'm going to have a nervous breakdown.'

While they were eating dinner, Joyce said to Albert.

'That dog is not well; he's pining.'

'Well, what should we do?'

'I don't know. He *has* to belong to someone somewhere,
and he wants to find them. Isn't there anything you can
do?'

Albert ate a huge lump of bread. 'Tricky,' he said.

'He's such a clever little chap.'

'So?'

'I mean, I bet someone is heartbroken at his disappearance.'

'Maybe.'

'Couldn't you stick a number on his collar?'

'Like what?'

'The telephone number of the police station or something.'

'That would be downright silly. Anyway, *if* anyone had the
sense to know it was a number of that sort, they'd just send the
poor little wretch back, wouldn't they?'

'Poor little wretch' – that's what I'd become, on the round-
abouts and swings like the gypsies had, but going nowhere, just
nowhere. I sat staring at the pale evening sunset, a dog that
walked alone with no real friends. I was overcome with a deep
loneliness. I was dead sorry for myself, which is not a good thing
to be. I should pull my finger right out and just go on trying to
find my way home, that's all there was to it. I was boring
myself, sitting there snivelling. All I wanted was to find my real
home, and sit with Them in the candle-lit evenings. Why, I'd
even look at this 'television'!

Silver and Sam lay stretched out on this patio.

'Eh up,' I said.

'What's that supposed to mean?' asked Silver.

'I don't know. It just came to me,' I answered. 'I think it's Yorkshire. I must have heard it a long time ago. I think it means how are you, or something like that.'

'Well, if you want to know, I have a bad sore throat,' said Sam.

'Don't give it to me,' Silver said, 'I hate sore throats with all my heart.'

'Me too,' I agreed. 'You need to gargle, and use some nose-drops. There's plenty of Kleenex in the loo.'

'Really! Imagine an Alsatian police dog using Kleenex! You must be potty!' And they both laughed.

I sat down beside them. I felt small, and I know I looked it – small, miserable and unwanted. Nobody spoke for some time. I had a good scratch, took a vague leak on a bit of box hedge, and came back to them.

'No one is going to thank you for spoiling the hedge,' Sam said.

'So what?' I answered rudely.

'I thought you were keen to get to your own place,' Silver said.

'Oh, I am, indeed I am, sir.'

'Well, we gave you the out, and what did you do? You came back here.'

'I know,' I said miserably. 'But honestly I could *not* stay in that poor lady's bed. It made me feel quite sick.'

'You should take off again.'

'I don't know where to take off to. I don't know where I am or which way to go. It's no use running round in circles.'

'You could go back to the wood and start from there. We could show you the way.'

'I don't want to go back to the wood, and anyway I was taken there in a van, so it wouldn't help. What's the name of this place anyway?'

'Amersham,' Sam said.

'Amersham?' Now, I'd heard of Amersham! P'raps I had

lived near it, or p'raps Mrs Punter, whom I used to stay with, lived there!

'Don't you know where you've lived?' asked Silver.

'Jamboree is all I can remember,' I replied.

'There is no such place,' said Sam. 'Believe me, we know practically everywhere, and Jamboree simply doesn't exist.'

'I live in a big house where the green grass goes on forever, and there is something called an azalea garden, and a vegetable garden, and a golden Caterpillar tree ...'

'Caterpillar tree!'

'And a tame gardener called Harold, and ...'

'Sounds like Windsor Castle,' laughed Sam.

'I don't think it was called that.'

'Well, your owners, what were they called?'

'Him and Her,' I replied.

'Everybody, but everybody, is called Him and Her. You're really not with it, not at all.'

'You'll have to get yourself together, Yapper.'

'You both seem to have forgotten that, first of all, my name is *not* Yapper; secondly, I have been lost and stolen, thirdly, I've been called a number of names.'

'I bet you have!' said Silver.

I hated him. 'My real name is Chips,' I said loftily.

'Listen,' said Sam, 'remember that you are supposed to be a terrier. Don't be so feeble, and moon around like a sick cat; we can point the way to Amersham roundabout and then you must just go on until you find something familiar.'

'Like a graveyard?' I asked.

'There are millions of those. I wouldn't waste my time on a graveyard. How about a pub?'

'I can't think of one, though I've been in some.'

'Well, you'd probably recognize one if you saw it,' he replied.

'Okay, where's the roundabout?'

'Personally, I don't see which exit he'd take,' Silver said.

'Well, he's just got to take a chance hasn't he? He'll probably end up by being stolen again anyway and given a new name. I don't like to be a defeatist, but I think he's a twerp not to stay here,' Sam said.

'I really don't want to stay here, though you're all so kind. But you two are away so much, and without being rude this *is* rather a small place. In any case, I don't like being beaten, even if I get stolen again.'

'It's a tough decision,' they both agreed.

'These Yorkies all look alike. He's got no collar for starters, and no distinguishing marks, far as I can see.'

'You all look alike too,' I replied.

'On the contrary, some of us are yellowish, some greyish. Not all of us are this magnificent black. Our owners would know us in a second, and we would certainly know them.'

'So would I!'

'They probably think you're dead, run over ...'

'My goodness!'

'Probably got another one by now anyway.'

My heart sank lower and lower. Suddenly, I just wished I was dead. I had taken life too easily, lolling about with Him and Her. I wished I'd been born an Alsatian that scared people. Then I remembered my ancestor, Huddersfield Ben, who fought monkeys and rats and was a great expert at bull-baiting. After all, I reminded myself, I *had* had a fight with this fox. I'll just have to keep going, even if I become a wanderer on the face of the earth. At least it'll be an adventure; at least it won't mean giving in and sitting around like a cat. Mean to say, I *have* adapted myself to most situations.

'Can't you give us a list of any names? It might help which exit you should take.'

'Well, Harold of course; Freddie, he's a squirrel; the man who brings the drink, the milkman; various Grand Sons; Mr Nagel ...'

'What a collection! You might as well have said Harrods and Fortnum & Mason!'

'They come to the house too!'

'They come to every house in the land, you twerp, even Buck House.'

'What's that?'

'You must be the most uneducated animal it's been our privilege to know,' Silver sniffed.

'I don't think I like your tone,' I answered bravely, because he *could* have bitten off my head, literally.

'Wait a minute! *Wait!*' shouted Sam.

'What?'

'This Mr Nagel – he rings a bell somewhere.'

'He's lame like me, and I go for his trousers,' I said excitedly, for dawn seemed to be breaking through the black clouds.

'Now, I don't know where he lives, but it's a sort of hut on some road ...' said Sam.

'Some help,' said Silver.

'All the same, it gives me an idea which exit to take, the one that leads across fields. You might have to go a long way. Think you can take such a journey?'

'Of course!'

'Right – let's go, Silver!'

We all got up stealthy-like. I followed them through the gate. Just as we were going, I heard this Joyce say, 'Albert, where are those boys going?'

'Move quickly,' said Sam.

To my horror I heard this big old Land-Rover starting up!

'What are you doing, Albert!' she asked.

'Following them,' he said. 'They're up to some lark. I'll call them to heel when I want to.'

We literally galloped down this road. My old injury hurt me but I kept up, and all the time I could see out of the tail of my eye this car following slowly behind.

We seemed to go for miles on these ghastly roads. People stopped and stared, and many laughed, but they kept well away from these two huge black dogs with me in the middle. Twice I thought I was going to faint, and it was getting dark as the sun was going down. And always behind us was this slow-moving police car. At one point it stopped and another policeman got in, which gave us a bit of a head start.

'I've got to stop!' I screamed.

'You can't.'

'My legs are shorter than yours, sir!'

They slowed down a bit.

'He's following, is Albert,' said Silver.

'Hope he doesn't call us in before we get to the roundabout,' panted Sam. 'Not far now, Yapper. You're doing well.'

I could have cried, hearing such a nice thing from this Great Dog. I mean Great in the sense of Greatness, because they could have got into trouble, doing this for me.

'Will he punish you?' I squawked.

'I think not. He trusts us, and he knows he can call us in with one whistle. Don't forget we *are* police dogs.'

'I won't,' I spluttered, 'but I think my heart will bust with this running. S'posing he picks me up too? Then it will be in vain, and I'll have killed myself.'

'He's watching to see what we do. Look, there's the roundabout! Just don't forget to yield to the traffic coming from the right.'

I didn't answer because I couldn't, and anyway I didn't know what he was talking about.

'Stay inbetween us and, when we say go, walk calmly. No car wants to run *us* over, I can tell you,' Sam said.

We waited on the edge of the road.

'Now,' said Sam.

I staggered over the road between them, glad to walk for a moment. Then, we were on this island-like thing.

'That is your exit to the left,' he said. 'Keep to the grass verge – it's better on the feet, and it don't waste time. We'll see you over, you're so small any car might think you are a rabbit.'

Again we crossed the road.

'Good luck, Yapper,' said Silver.

'You're really a brave little cuss, a proper terrier.'

I could hardly see them for the tears running out of my eyes. I sat down on the grass verge and watched them cross to this island-thing, and off it to the other side. The police car had stopped, and Albert and the other policeman got out and stood waiting. Sam and Silver, with their tails wagging like flags, ran towards them. The police never moved, and if they said anything I couldn't have heard it.

'Carry on, Sergeant,' Sam barked.

I crawled a few yards and sat down again, trying to catch my breath. Still they all stood watching.

'Turn into the next field and keep going. You might see a pub you know, but try not to get caught again. Use your teeth,' Silver barked furiously.

I dragged myself along and pretty soon saw a way into this field. There were these big black and white animals in it but they only stared at me. I looked back. They were all still standing there. Then these great boys got into the car, which turned round and went back the way it had come.

I had lost two of my best friends and I lay down in the grass with exhaustion. My body shook all over; I think it's called sobbing ... After a while I pulled up my socks and started off into the unknown. Sometimes the grass was too high to see where I was going and, as I didn't know anyway, I just kept straight on. I must have gone for miles. My coat was full of burrs and fleas and wet all over, so I must have looked like a rat. I prayed no one would shoot me.

I came on a road and saw an open rubbish-bin. I wondered whether to spend the night in it, but then I thought someone might pour some more rubbish on top of me and I'd be taken to a dump, so I lay down behind a tree and fell asleep.

The birds woke me – a couple of Kòo Koos – and I cried again, glad the Boys couldn't see me. I blundered on. I was really hungry, but I'd learned not to go near any houses. Then, horror of horrors, a milk-float stopped beside me.

'Going my way, mate?' the milkman asked. I knew he was a milkman because he wore the same clothes as the one I used to go for. He got out. I bared my teeth at him and barked, but I seemed to have lost my voice a bit.

'You poor little wreck,' he said. 'You look starved to death!'

He went back to the van and brought out a bowl, and poured some milk into it with some bread. I went for it like a madman.

'There now, that's better, ain't it, mate? You're lost, that's what you are.'

I wagged what was left of my tail feebly.

'Can't just go away and leave you here, can I, mate? Better take you to the police station.'

Police Station? Which one, and how many of them were there? I remembered about this Pound the man had told Her Grace about! That would be the end of me. I'd probably be there for years! I started to run, but I fell over. He came over to me and I bit his trousers.

'Understandable, chum,' he said and picked me up. I was too weak to fight any more. He carried me to his milk-float and rubbed me all over with his coat.

'That's better, matie. Now we can see what you is. You're a Yorkie, a lost Yorkie. You spend the day with me and we'll see what happens.' He wrapped me in his coat and rumbled on. I fell asleep.

This milkman drove his milk-float round endless roads and endless houses. I was asleep most of the time, thinking and dreaming of my friends: Him and Her of course, but also my animal friends who had helped me, like Wellington and Barmy, and especially the two police dogs, those magnificent black beauties. I was sad to think I'd never see them again, and I knew too I'd never be young again. I felt sick to my stomach.

'Lunch-time, matie,' he said suddenly. 'We'll pop into this here pub and get a bite each, bit of beer p'raps.'

I looked up with red-rimmed, sore eyes. We had arrived at this pub – the Dumbell. Surely I knew the Dumbell! I seemed to remember going there with Them and looking at some nasty dangerous ghosts with horns. I must be near something or somewhere I knew. I barked happily and followed the milkman into this pub. 'Look out for a pub you remember', Silver had said. I squeezed inbetween his legs as we went through the door.

'Morning, Ted,' he said.

'Morning, Len. Wot you got there then?'

'Lost Yorkie. Found him miles away. Starved, he were.'

'Quite good-looking,' a man said.

'Did you see the picture in the *Sun* of some Yorkie what identified that criminal Johnson? Looks just like him,' said another.

'Well, they all looks alike, don't they? Clever dogs mind you, good circus dogs, teach 'em anything. Got a collar 'as 'e?'

'No identification,' answered my friend. 'Better take him to the police station at Tatling End.'

'My missus would like 'im, you can tell 'em. She lost one t'other day. Run over by a clumsy long vehicle.'

Suddenly I saw *him*! The weirdo Harold! He was sitting on a stool with his legs swinging and laughing! I rushed up to him shouting the same old ruderies, and jumping up and down on his trousers!

''Ullo? What's this then?' he asked.

' 'E either knows you, or 'e don't like you!' someone laughed.

'We had one of them once,' said Harold. 'The Governor was mad keen on him. He used to take him to the golf course.'

I went on barking furiously.

'He never took to me, don't know why. But he got hisself lost or stole. They was ever so upset.'

'Don't you recognize 'im then?'

'Well, they all looks alike to me.'

I went on barking and jumping. He drained his beer.

'No distinguishing marks?' someone asked.

'No. Anyway, he looks such a mess.'

By now I was more than frantic. My last chance, and this idiot couldn't recognize me. I wished I hadn't been so rude to him in the past.

'What were 'e called?'

'Chips, that's what he was called.'

I flung myself round in circles. I lay on the floor. I went for his trousers!

'That's what he did last time!' He leaned toward me. 'Chips?' he asked.

I jumped up on to his lap and licked his face all over.

'Well!' he said, holding me in his arms. 'He had one bad leg, the right one, broke it when he was a puppy.' He held me away from him and looked me in the eye, this man who knew more about flowers and birds than anyone.

'Chips,' he said, 'if you've got one bad leg, you hold it up for me to see.'

I lifted my right arm.

'That's him,' he said.

'Well, blow me down,' someone said. 'Clever as monkeys.'

'How to get him back? I've only got my bike,' said Harold.

'How about you, Len?' somebody asked.

'I've got to finish me round in the opposite direction,' he replied.

'I could get him there tonight,' Ted said.

'It's my bike,' Harold told them. 'Can't wait for my bike till tonight.'

'Why can't you take him on your bike?' Len asked.

Harold threw his eyes to Heaven in a familiar gesture. 'He won't sit quiet on that! He'd have me in the mud in no time!' And he laughed uproariously.

'And you wouldn't want to breathe in a bag after what you consumed!' They all thought this hilarious.

I sat quietly on Harold's lap, licking his face hopefully.

'Looks quiet enough,' said Len. 'He's dead tired. Come on, I got an old coat you can tie him on with.'

Still laughing, Harold allowed the two of us to be taken to his old bike. He got himself on to it. Len made a sort of bag of his coat into which I most obediently collapsed.

'Now, what we does is this: put his little paws round your neck and I'll tie him round you.'

'Oh, oh,' Harold laughed, 'won't be long before I'm off, specially if he keeps turning his head left and right. Might not like travelling backwards.'

'Get along. Be a sport.' They all crowded round laughing. I sat absolutely still.

'Can't see through all his hair!' Harold shouted, as we peddled dangerously away.

'Good boy,' they all shouted and we were off.

Well, I have to admit I was terrified. If I jump, I thought, I'll kill myself. My only hope of getting home now was with Harold. I never moved, but Harold was laughing so much we nearly collided with a car. He swerved and landed in a mound of garbage stuff. He had his trousers covered in muck, and apple-pulp in his ears, and his brown cap was covered in some rice-pudding. He sat on the ground still laughing and rubbing his elbows. I was tired and smelly and still strapped round his neck in this old coat.

'Now, look where we are,' he grunted. 'Can't seem to get these arms untied. Not hurt, are you, Chips?'

I licked his filthy cap. Then, very cleverly I thought, I wriggled out of the coat, and stood wagging my tail at him.

'The front wheel is bent on top of everything else,' he muttered. He put his face in his hands – thinking, I s'pose.

'We got to walk, that's about the size of it,' he was talking to himself, I could see that. 'Murderous, that's what it is.'

I barked hopefully, ran ahead and then came back to him.

'It's not far if you think you can stay by me. I'll tie you to the back wheel.'

He got a piece of string out of his pocket – he always had string on him – and put it round my neck. Then he picked up this tangled bike and tried to move it. It wouldn't move.

'That's done it,' he grumbled.

No way would this horrible machine move. He sat down in the mud. I sat beside him. No matter what happened I wasn't going to leave his side. He tried to get the rice-pudding off his cap; he really looked a ghastly sight.

Then I saw the old familiar police car zooming along towards us.

'That's torn it,' he said in a sort of scared way.

The police car stopped by us and a policeman got out. 'Bit of trouble?' he asked.

Harold could only nod.

'What happened?'

'Well sir, I was trying to carry my dog home and a car near ran me down, so I fell into all this muck.'

'Rather a silly experiment, if you ask me. You sure it's your dog?'

'Oh yes, sir. Aren't you, Chips?'

I barked and wagged my tail.

'I think you've had one or twelve over the eight, if you ask me,' said the policeman.

'Oh no, sir, only the half pint of Mackeson!'

'Well, you won't get this vehicle to move. Better put it in the back, and I'll take you home.'

I barked happily.

'He's not going to snap at me, is he?'

'Never, sir. Never snaps at no one!'

They struggled together to get the bent thing in.

'Phew, you smell like a brewery.'

'I do, sir?'

'You most certainly do. I ought to book you.'

Harold looked most crestfallen. I could see he was trying not to breathe.

'Go on, get in, you miserable sight.'

'Lucky the flaming car didn't kill us,' he muttered inaudibly.

'Where were you going?'

'To my employers' house, sir, in the village.' Him and Her!

No more was said, and we sailed back into my long lost Paradise! I was home! We stopped at the familiar white gates. I could hardly believe my eyes; I felt ten years younger! I jumped up and down and scratched at the gates while they got this mangled affair out.

'Thank you, sir,' said Harold. 'They'll be so happy. You see he's been lost and they've been grieving.' Together they carted the thing in and stood it against the garage door.

'Now you be a good boy, and don't let me catch you again.'

'No, sir.'

'And get washed up.' Then he drove away.

Harold limped to the kitchen door and unlocked it. I flew in, barking wildly. There was no one there. Only silence.

'And don't you leave this here kitchen, that there burglar thing will let orf. They're out, that's where they are.'

I was so disappointed I could have screamed the house down. I looked round. My basket had gone; They *had* forgotten me. My drinking and eating bowls had gone too! No sign of any of Them that I had known, not one of them. I sat on the floor. Harold started to wash himself. Then he gave me a saucer of milk. I felt too sick to look at it.

'Hey,' he said, suddenly. 'You need a wash too.'

I didn't care any more. I had expected everyone to come rushing with shouts of joy. Where were They?

Harold turned on the water in the basin and put me in. Then he got hold of this fairy liquid and poured it all over me. I let him. He dried me with a couple of tea towels. I let him.

'That's a good boy. That's a good Chips.'

It was very cold in this dear old kitchen, and I shivered. I'm going to die of bronchitis, that's what I'm going to do, I thought.

'Better come to the Swan for a bit,' Harold said.

He looked in the drawer for some string, I s'pose, but he didn't find it, and the leads weren't hanging up on the door any more. They'd definitely given me up forever; probably got that setter she wanted. Well, that's life.

He carried me to the Swan. His brother Ken was waiting for him.

'Isn't that Chips?' he asked, astonished-like.

'It is, and a good old time we've had getting here.'

'He's very docile. Sure it's the right dog?'

'I think he's fed up,' said Harold, putting his face into this huge glass of black stuff.

The girl behind the bar looked at me. 'That looks like Chips,' she said.

'It is. Found him at the Dumbell.'

'Well I never! Soaking wet too; needs a blow dry.'

We were alone so she got this 'blow dry' out and warmed me up. There was no one I could ask questions. I just sat there miserably.

'Looks poorly to my way of thinking,' she said. 'And if he's the dog what identified that man he's a blinking hero.'

'Could be,' Harold said. 'Could be easy.'

'Reckon he is, too,' said Ken.

Well, I listened while Harold went into the whole story. It was good to be back, but s'pose they had another dog now and loved him more than me? Of course I couldn't ask Harold, though I'll never know why he can't understand animals, he knows so much about them birds.

They got up at last because Harold wanted to show his bike to Ken. They laughed a lot on the way home. He forgot to pick me up so I just trotted behind quietly.

'Changed, hasn't he?' said Harold.

'They do, you know,' Ken said.

I couldn't stand the kitchen. Mean to say, it was lifeless really. I drank some water and went outside. What a dismal arrival. What an anti-climax.

'Come on,' said Harold. 'We'll give them a lovely surprise, always s'posing you're the right dog!' And he laughed again. 'You come down to the strawberry bed and hide, and then when they come back, you bark a coupla times, and then we'll see.'

I sat beside the strawberry bed as Harold had told me and watched all these birds fly round me. There was one of the Koo Koos coming right up to me, quite tame, with no fear, because She fed them every day, and so did Harold. One is a widow, which is sad: he hit his head on an apple tree, and now she has to fly round alone. Everybody, but everybody should have a mate, that's the way it was arranged by 'you know who', though I don't really know who 'who' is. I just know there has to be someone – mean to say, someone arranged this beautiful garden. Maybe it's Harold! Mean to say, the Koo Koos follow him about and Fred walks behind him like a dog. He is as thin as a knife, but that doesn't mean much. His eyes are as blue as the sky, and so are His while Hers are green, and Her hair is like the sunlight. P'raps heaven, or whatever they call it, after all, is just this fantastic garden, and I have to thank my dear friends I was back in it, safely by the strawberry bed.

'Hullo,' said a voice.

I looked over my shoulder. It was Fred!

'Have you come back?' he asked.

'I can understand your language, Fred!' I said.

'That's because you've learned to,' he said. 'That means you won't chase me anymore.'

'It certainly doesn't,' I answered. 'When I'm better!'

'How did you find the way back?' he asked. 'Finding the way back isn't easy.'

'I came back on a milk-float,' I replied.

'One kind of float is as good as another,' Fred answered. He sat up on his hind feet with his two hands together on his chest above his white apron.

'Harold can't see me anymore you know because I'm dead. This cat got me.'

'It can't be true!' I gasped. 'You must have made a mistake!'

'Well, nothing is really *dead*, is it?' he asked. 'It's a question of if you can see and understand.'

I thought I was going to faint among the snowflakes.

Harold drove his Wheel Horse up to us. He didn't seem to notice Fred, who laughed and ran away.

'They're coming,' he said, though I don't know how he knew.

'Hide behind the four yew trees, and keep quiet,' he said.

I did just that. I heard the clang of the garage doors. I heard the car come in. I bit my lip to stop myself crying out.

'You shut up,' said Harold and walked away.

I could hear Their voices! It was hard to believe! Then suddenly I could bear it no longer and I started barking. I could see Them through the trees. She stopped suddenly and turned to Him.

'Surely I heard him,' She said.

'Don't be so Celticly idiotic. You're like Mrs Darling in Peter Pan who thought she heard the children's voices! How sentimental can you get,' and He turned away.

'But I've got better hearing and sight than you!' She remonstrated.

'I want some tea,' He said. 'I'll make it.'

Harold gave me the nod, and I flew along to the kitchen and stood in the doorway, Harold behind me. She was putting the kettle on. She turned and saw him.

'Hullo, Harold dear,' She said.

We didn't move. She stared for a moment and then snatched at her black glasses. She sees better with them. She stared disbelievingly at me.

'Harold,' She said. 'Are you alone?'

'No, M'Lady,' he answered.

We stared at each other. She ran out of the door calling, 'Darling, darling, I've seen a ghost!'

They came back and saw me. He's not Celtic, just English, so He's more on the ball.

'Chips,' He said in a small voice. 'Chips?'

I flung myself at Him barking anxiously, jumping up and down and catching His fingers in my mouth without biting, as I used to do. He picked me up and hugged me.

'Oh Chips!' He said. 'Our Adventurer is back! It's Chips all right, he's come home!'

She fell on Her knees cuddling me to Her, tears streaming down Her face. She couldn't speak, just kept shaking Her head and sniffling in big gulps. He looked at Harold.

'It's a long story, sir. He came to the Dumbell on a milk-float. Where he's been no one will ever know 'cos he can't tell us can he? Brought him back on my bike and we had a bit of rough and tumble with a car in the lanes. Afraid the bike is a write 'orf and . . .'

'We'll buy you another, Harold darling,' She said.

'We was both in a mess, but we both had a good wash and just waited. He's changed a lot. Quite docile really, jest follered Ken and me from the Swan with no lead, and sat down by the strawberry bed till I told him to go. Reckon he's a lot older.'

'Dearest,' She said to Him, 'get his dear old basket out of the garage. Poor little darling, he looks half-starved.'

He went off to the garage and got out my glamorous basket with the white rug. He put it down and I got into it.

'And now he's going to have half our cold chicken,' She said.

I really wasn't hungry, I was too tired to eat, but I stuffed myself till I nearly burst. Then I had a long drink of water, then I rushed round the house like a maniac to all the old and familiar places.

'Oh Dearest, he's back again,' He said and They hugged each other. 'Everyone has gone, and it's just you and me and him, like it used to be!'

'I'm afraid we've lost Fred,' She told me sadly. 'We never see him any more, he must have had an accident.'

'He hasn't! He hasn't!' I shouted, 'I've just talked to him in the snow.'

She scooped me up. 'Isn't he sweet!' She said. 'If only we

could understand what he's on about,' He said. 'He seems to have so much to say.'

If only you could, I thought.

It was like old times in the library before dinner: games, laughs and talks in front of the fire, and all those familiar smells. I put my feet up on the wall of Disgrace Corner and thought about myself; I looked back and remembered, making new resolutions, like not being quite so beastly to Harold, or Mr Nagel, or biting ankles, leaking on chairs, digging up the lawn, eating all the apron strings, to be more benevolent, tolerant and calmer.

You have to suffer some things, however small, to mature; you have to see how other people live, and how kind mostly they are to each other. I'll never forget any of the ones I met, ever; and that fox – how sorry I am he was so hungry, and those assassinated chickens, who were only minding their business.

I reckon I'm lucky, but it's not going to be easy to get me to go beyond the garden; I couldn't take a chance on all those hazards again. Only one thing, I'd like to find Barmy and Wellington, and those two black beauties who showed me the right exit. Seems to me it's all a question of taking the right exit in the end.

I ate a light supper of a cheese sandwich, took a leak on the caterpillar tree, and then we all went to bed, with me in the middle. I lay on my back listening to Them talking, staring through the windows at the snowflakes, white against the black sky and skeleton trees. I could hear the roosting sounds of all the birds that made Albert unhappy because he never saw them anymore. They are safe here, I thought, because they've nowt to fear – nowt. That's Yorkshire, and I've said it for the first time!

I wish I could have told Them where I'd been and what I'd seen. I wish I could make Them understand that Fred was still running round the garden if They could only see.

I started listening to Their conversation. He was saying how sad it was about some friend of Theirs.

'We must never be apart again ever,' She said.

'Right.'

'We must live every day as if it were our last.'

'Right.'

'You never know, do you?' She pondered.

'No, you never know when something awful might happen, a sudden end to it all,' He said.

There was silence for a moment and They stroked me lying between Them.

'You know what thought always upsets me terribly?' She asked.

'No?'

'Their spectacles. Just lying there with no eyes looking through.'

'Oh! What a ghastly thought,' He said and laughed.

I imagine They were talking about Fred. But Fred never wore spectacles. I didn't hear any more. I fell blissfully asleep.